FIRST EXPERIENCE

A Beginner's Guide to Owning and Caring for Horses

by

SIOUX DALLAS

CCB Publishing
British Columbia, Canada

First Experience:
A Beginner's Guide to Owning and Caring for Horses

Copyright ©2012 by Sioux Dallas
ISBN-13 978-1-927360-98-9
First Edition

Library and Archives Canada Cataloguing in Publication
Dallas, Sioux, 1930-
First experience : a beginner's guide to owning and caring for horses /
written by Sioux Dallas ; Foreword by William S. Biddle – 1st ed.
ISBN 978-1-927360-98-9
Also available in electronic format.
Additional cataloguing data available from Library and Archives Canada

Publisher: CCB Publishing
             British Columbia, Canada
             www.ccbpublishing.com

DEDICATED TO THE MEMORY OF MY HUSBAND

FRANCIS GROVE MICHAEL DALLAS

Who encouraged me and helped me with all phases of
my work so that I would be free to write.

Books Written by Sioux Dallas

First Experience

Sharon

Desperate Wish

L i i s a

Death in Three Quarter Time

The Perfect Spouse

Montana Madness

Dangerous Hilarity

Amish Dilemma

And coming soon:

A Detective's Heart

Amish Promise

The Snowman Murder

I am mounted on a three-year-old Shire stallion which I helped to train. His name was Ladbrook Jock and he was nineteen point two hands tall. He leveled off at twenty-one point two hands when fully grown.

He was bred to a beautiful big Thoroughbred mare. The result was a wonderful colt that reached seventeen point two hands; looked like his sire and had a sweet temperament. He's being ridden as a heavy hunter.

Jock was brought from England at ten months of age. When the plane door was opened and he was led to the opening, he looked out over our country and neighed loudly as if to say, "All right you lucky people, I'm here." He was a sweetheart with which to work. He had lovely, smooth gaits and a willing disposition. I fell in love.

CONTENTS

FOREWORD
by
Major General William S. Biddle

Several years ago, the pleasure of owning a riding horse belonged mainly to the comparatively rich. In the past few years, however, the possibility of horse ownership has become a hobby for any person who wished to be part of the "horse crowd".

With good pasture and fresh water, there were relatively few problems in caring for an equine. Today, due to dense population and congested traffic, a horse owner, or handler, has many responsibilities to the animal. The horse will be only as healthy and manageable as the person who cares for him will make it possible.

Sioux Dallas has high praise for several outstanding authors. She and I agree, however, that the majority of the better books are written so that one must have some previous knowledge on the subject before the material can be useful to the reader.

Sioux has written a delightfully refreshing book that will be useful especially to persons who have never owned a horse. She deals with easily understood basic fundamentals that will be helpful to the novice and the amateur.

Sioux has instructed people of all ages and on all levels of ability. Some of her students have progressed to successful showing in major rated shows. Some were blind and mentally challenged. She gave sensitive care and consideration to each person equally because of her sincere regard for people and for animals. All, to whom I have spoken, regard her highly for her integrity and her compassion.

I like Sioux's philosophy that anyone can be successful if he or she cares to exert the necessary effort and the time required to do well. She feels success is what each individual wants for himself or herself and each must face his or her own conscience in striving to reach standards and goals.

This book is written so that a prospective owner can know the full responsibilities, the financial obligations, the assets and liabilities BEFORE purchasing a horse. With this knowledge a person can select a mount and a stable more wisely.

To be forearmed will help the person in an understanding relationship with the animal so that each can enjoy working to the fullest with the other.

Each reader will find something useful and something enjoyable in this book. The illustrations add a great deal, but Sioux's personal experiences, some humorous and some serious, add more than pictures or pages of facts. This material is entirely from her own experiences and knowledge which she has gained through the years.

William S. Biddle

Maj. Gen. William S. Biddle

Picture of Maj. Gen. Biddle

PREFACE

This book has been written with a great deal of love and agony. The information in it is of my own experience and is not intended to be the answer to all problems. To cover each subject in detail would require a book too heavy and expensive. I only hope that millions of people can love and enjoy their horses as I have, and will be encouraged by my experiences.

This is not a book that will teach a person how to ride or all the steps to train a horse. It is to prepare a person to assume the responsibility of caring for an animal so that person and animal are happy, healthy, and safe.

My primary purpose is to make prospective horse and pony owners aware of common problems so that they will be safe and do well. Hopefully they will also be to be more psychologically ready to own an equine and know the financial responsibilities involved. It is simple to buy an animal, but the daily maintenance is sometimes more than some can accept. Also, if more people were aware of the physical and emotional involvement, there would be fewer neglected animals and fewer injured, disillusioned humans. Animals have feeling, also.

Nothing replaces one's own experiences which takes years and more hard work than many realize. However, all of us can learn from others through observation and reading. We never stop learning. One person's workable solution may not suit the exact need of another's, but it can serve as a guide. Personalities of all humans differ, and animals are the same. Therefore, one type of training will not be successful on all equines. Be patient, but firm, kind and consistent. You'll need to experiment to find the best approach for you in dealing with that individual animal.

Although basic knowledge, patience, consistency, love and firmness are imperative, they are worthless without common sense. There is an old saying, "Experience is the best school, and fools learn in no other."

How true I have found this to be. Another saying, "A little knowledge is dangerous," is factual in the equine world. Those who have a few lessons, or work with an animal for a short time, sometimes think they are a natural. Those individuals can look forward to ruining good horse flesh, getting themselves hurt, or causing harm to others. There are also those who own horses and ride for years but never become a horseperson -- just a passenger.

I can give an excellent example. We were having a 4-H horse show at a county park. A fourteen-year-old girl, apparently, had always had whatever she wanted. Between classes she went into the ring and ran her horse around and around until he was sweating. She grinned as if she had done something outstanding. She finally took a friend up behind her and they ran more. She knew nothing about leads or how to guide the horse. She had just gotten on the horse with no lessons. I heard a crack and heard the horse scream. He fell to the ground with the left front leg broken. Wrong lead. Thrashing around he broke the other leg. The park ranger refused to put him down and out of his misery. I begged him to loan me his pistol so I could do it, but he refused until the veterinarian came to put the animal down. A good, young, healthy horse was lost and the girls risked injury to themselves because they had little knowledge and little common sense. I blamed the parents.

It would be impossible to name all the individuals who aided me while I was learning. I'm thankful for the many kind ones who were willing to share their knowledge and experiences so that I could learn correctly and safely. I also attended some good training schools.

Sadly some people gain knowledge and experience, then forget that they were once beginners and needed help. They are often resentful of a 'newcomer'. Fortunately I have made many wonderful friends who were happy to share.

Don't let age or limited physical ability hold you back. If you truly are willing to devote the time and effort, you CAN LEARN. Some may need more time than others. That does not mean their goal is unreachable. Some do not care to ride, but are happy working with animals on the ground and helping other. There will be down days and everyone gets discouraged at times. Stay with it. Time and experience will make a tremendous difference. Age, weight and disability should never hold one back. I learned and YOU CAN, TOO.

Actually this could apply to anything in life in which one is interested.

POINTS TO PONDER

A specific breed, or a big price, does not necessarily mean a quality horse. The first point to consider is the temperament of the animal. Do have a <u>qualified</u> person with you to select a horse. Consider the training of the animal and the person. Never place an untrained person with a young, untrained, or partially trained animal unless they will have a qualified trainer working with them. Consider where the animal will be kept and the amount of daily attention he will receive.

After you've found the horse you want, pay a qualified veterinarian to give the animal a good physical. Have a written contract stating what you expect from the animal and what you plan to do. Keep this and the receipt for purchase in a safe place.

Regardless of the type of friendship (or relation) never allow anyone to ride or handle your horse unless that person is trained and can conduct themselves with common sense. Remember: A FRIEND TODAY MAY NOT BE A FRIEND TOMORROW. Also, in today's society there are far too many who are eager to sue for any reason. That goes with the old saying, "Three people can keep a secret if two of them are dead."

<u>Have good insurance on your horse to cover any injury to the animal or to anyone else as well as damage to other's</u>

property. Have a good farrier (blacksmith) on a regular basis.

Ladies and gentlemen, keep long hair up in braids or in a net. Long hair flapping around gives the appearance of being unsteady in the saddle and makes the rider look sloppy. It makes the horse look as if he has an undesirable gait. Additionally, the hair could swing in front of the eyes at a critical moment and contribute to an accident.

Ladies, wear a good support bra. The bouncing not only looks ugly but can damage muscles and cause the bust to droop.

A hard-soled shoe, especially with a heel, is a must. It not only is easier on the feet, but will help keep the foot from sliding into the stirrup too far and getting caught if the rider should happen to come off. Keep your heels slightly down and the iron (stirrup) on the ball of the foot -- English or Western. I ride English, Western and side saddle, and am very careful with my feet in the stirrup.

A helmet or hard hat is a must for all beginners or when training a young horse.

NEVER run your horse on a hard surface. If it is necessary to travel along or across the highway, either walk well off the hard surface or get off and lead. Do not ride double in the open. Stay alert on the road because there are some silly people who think it is funny to blow their horn or yell out the window and make a horse jump.

On a long ride, allow the horse to rest about every hour or so. Either get off and walk for a short distance and lead or stop. If you stop, loosen the girth to allow air under the saddle and to make the animal comfortable. Check the horse's feet for a stone or injury. Always remember to tighten the girth before you remount.

NEVER SHOW OFF. A person who is a good rider does not have to show off. His or her performance speaks for itself.

READY

KICK A TIRE!

TRY THE HORN!

CHECK THE BRAKES!

INSPECT
THE UNDERSISDE

Of course no one would buy a car using only these tests. Yet I am continuously amazed at people who use similar methods to buy a horse. They have their heart set on a color or a breed that has been in the movies or that someone else owns. Some want a mount that can run fast or jump without realizing the training required for these actions and the rider's training for guiding the animal.

Consideration should be given to the experience and the knowledge of the person who will be riding and handling the animal. Do get lessons from a qualified person, not just a friend or neighbor who happens to get on a horse and pretends to ride. Many people have called me to help them in the selection of a horse for their child (or themselves). I ask about the riding experience and the answer I most often receive is, "Oh, she doesn't ride yet, but she reads a lot and loves horses."

Don't misunderstand me. I am not putting down reading or love for the sport. But, wow! One might as well say, "My son doesn't know how to ride a bull, but I'm getting him one because he is crazy about rodeo cowboys."

Just because the horse moves with a rider on his back doesn't mean there is no responsibility on the part of the human. That equine is not a machine, but a living, breathing being with a mind of its own. Sometimes its thoughts require a person's stout heart and strong willpower. If one doesn't know how to react to a horse's actions, there can be disaster waiting. Their minds are about equal to a good three-year-old child.

Before you decide to buy, ask yourself if you are prepared to rise early each morning to give the time and effort required for daily care. It's good if you have a capable, qualified person ready and willing to advise. Even if you think you have some knowledge, you will be surprised at what you do not know as you progress. None of us become so perfect that there's nothing left to learn. You will be a teacher every time you touch the animal or are around it. The memory of the average horse is good, so make sure your handling leaves valuable and pleasant memories.

Habits and memories are given to an equine by the person handling him. His actions, instinctive to run, remains in the horse from thousands of years ago. Therefore, it is the responsibility of the person to know what she or he is doing and to be considerate of the feelings of the animals. They even get backaches and headaches.

Enjoy your equine to a ripe old age by having enough common sense to admit that you need help and guidance, and are willing to be taught and corrected. It is vitally important that the person helping you is knowledgeable, patient and willing. Learning to ride and care properly for a horse is not easy, nor is it learned quickly. However, the rewards are worth all of the blood, sweat and tears.

I must strongly urge that lessons be taken from a reputable person or a licensed establishment. Please don't depend on free help from a friend or neighbor just because they own a horse or have been on top of one. An honest person will never object if you question their ability.

It has been said that the outside of a horse is good for the inside of a person. I can testify to that. A quiet ride early in the morning can be refreshing and help sooth personal problems. When feeling low or discouraged, just listen to the nickers of welcome and hug a horse's neck. That will boost the ole spirits. After grooming the animal and cleaning the stall, you will find that a lot of frustration and tension is gone, or does not seem as serious. My personal opinion is that even if one does not ride, just being around the animal, or as I do, singing or talking to them will be of therapeutic value. My Cherokee loved to have me sing to him and place his name in the song.

Keep in mind that there is more than the purchase price. You'll have the daily expense of food, vitamins, tools, grooming equipment, feeding tubs, water buckets, blankets for cold weather and many other items. Tack, which is saddle and bridle, your clothing and treats, will all be necessary. The saddle must be cleaned every time it is used; the bridle must be washed and hung up properly, brushes must be cleaned and kept in a particular place, including hoof pick, feeding tubs must be washed each time and water buckets must be emptied, cleaned and filled with fresh water. Put all grooming supplies away at their assigned spot.

You can plan on regular medical expenses (veterinarian check-ups), farrier, shelter, hay, feed, worming, teeth floated and checking every day for possible injuries, temperature and just being alert. If your horse gets sick or injured, there is additional care. You will need first aid supplies and know how to use them. In the event you care to show, there are special clothes, entry fees, traveling and medical papers to take with you. There are also required shots for several diseases.

Can you fit all this into your budget and time? Are you willing to give the necessary effort required every day for a happy, healthy mount? If so ----

GET SET

Check the facilities. Will the horse be boarded on your property or will you pay for board? In either case, is there someone to assume the care of daily grooming, checking feet, feeding, exercising or training, making sure there is a salt lick, fresh water and that no one bothers or steals your animal? Make sure no one will ride, or mistreat, your animal when you are not around.

If boarding away from home, investigate the place thoroughly. Sometimes the boarding place learns the habits of the owner and will rent out your horse if they know you're not going to be around. Sometimes even though they've agreed to feed and groom, they will not do this. Have a written agreement as to what you expect and what they will promise to do. Go by at odd times so they won't know when to expect you and make sure your animal is being cared for.

I had a healthy, beautiful mare and colt that I had to leave with two men because I had a broken arm. I left plenty of feed and they promised to groom and feed and care for them. I went in unexpected just four days later and the horses were frantic. They had not been fed and had lost an alarming amount of weight. They were grubby looking and upset. The colt reared up and cut his head on an overhead beam. I suspected they had been ridden in the wrong way.

Is there good shelter to protect from hard rain or high winds and intense sun? Does each horse have its own place without crowding or allowing another horse to steal their feed?

Are there dangerous pieces of machinery, broken glass, protruding nails, splinters or trash around that would be an unsafe environment?

Are there too many animals crowding causing irritability, fights and other dangerous practices? Disease and infections will spread rapidly with overcrowding. Is there enough quality pasture and will a balanced hay be fed? Is fresh water available at all times? Is a salt block provided? Is the fencing sturdy and safe?

Is the pasture a good nutritional grass that is cared for and seeded when necessary? Just green things growing could be weeds with no food value. Is the manure spread or picked up? If manure is left in the pasture, paddock or stalls, there is greater danger of parasites, infections and serious health problems. Urine contains ammonia that can burn the skin and eyes. If urine and manure are left in the stalls, this can cause serious skin problems.

Years ago my veterinarian advised me to keep cobwebs off the stall walls and ceilings. The web gathers a film of dust which is a major cause of respiratory problems in older horses or very young ones. An old folk tale is that the webs will gather flies, mosquitoes, etc. This is not healthy. I keep an old broom and keep the stall walls clean, constantly sweeping down webs and beehives.

Are there splintered boards, wires or nails in the stall or paddock area that might be dangerous? Will the feeding tub and water bucket be washed daily? Dirty feeding tubs attract germs and insects. If a wooden box is built in the corner of the stall for feeding, then place a rubber tub in it so that it can be washed.

If there is pasture boarding with no stalls, will each animal be tied by its own bucket for feeding? If not, the bullies will take the feed and starve the timid ones. It's possible that the underdog might develop a defensive attitude even toward humans if he has to fight for his feed.

Put yourself in the horse's place. How would you like to try to eat with someone pushing you away and taking the food and not allowing you to eat in peace? If feeding flakes of hay in the open, place two more flakes than the number of horses. If the bullies chase the timid ones away from the hay, there is always flake of hay.

Is there adequate room to exercise or train your horse? Will there be a safe area in the field for riding, or luckily a ring? Are there trails for pleasure riding or to reward your horse after a training session?

If you have to furnish training equipment such as jumps, poles or barrels, will your equipment be kept in a safe place? Will other boarders share the expense with you and help keep the equipment in good, safe shape?

To have an animal in your care is a great responsibility. Like a small child, the horse is willing to trust you and work with you as long as you give the proper care and attention. How that animal grows and learns will depend on you. You CAN teach an old dog new tricks with time and patience. That also goes for horses.

Are you still interested and enthused? Great!!! Then ----

Go

Consult a capable, knowledgeable, trustworthy person to help you decide on the best mount for you and the stable. The temperament of both the animal and the rider must be considered. Training of both mount and rider is most important. How tall is the rider as compared to the height of the horse? Is the weight too much for that particular horse or pony or is the rider not going to be strong enough to handle a spirited mount? What are the final goals of the rider? What do you plan to do with the horse? For instance one cannot make a jumper out of a Tennessee Walker. Neither can one expect to make a good timed event horse out of one with a straight shoulder.

If you just want to love your horse for pleasure riding, then look for a wise, dependable mount, even one with a little age. An aged gelding is excellent for a beginning rider. If you intend to work with a 4-H group, you will need a younger, stronger, more even-tempered, healthy and willing horse.

If you have completed a reasonable amount of training and expect to compete in showing events, you will need an animal according to the use you expect from him.

Ponies are dearly loved, and, too often, quickly outgrown. Very few can bear to part with them, thus an added expense. It's possible to teach the pony to pull a cart. Those little rascals are smart and strong-minded. Often it takes a person with a firm hand and more strength and experience than a smaller person to handle a pony.

Please note that I have not recommended a particular breed. This is like people. You should never lump an entire race of people on an opinion based upon your experience with one of them. I feel that this is as personal as choosing your own toothbrush or clothing. I do strongly advise getting a good, healthy gelding until you have more training. A stallion is a NO NO for the average person unless you have a trainer who will handle him for breeding. A mare can be just as temperamental to handle as a stallion when she is in season (ready to breed).

A stallion has a specific purpose in life and should only be handled by persons trained to handle them. He can be a joy to ride if he has been trained to be a gentleman under tack, but look out if a mare in season comes near.

I beg of you, don't be foolish enough to think it sounds great to say you have a stallion just because you fell in love with a movie version. After all, horses such as Fury, Black Jack, Black Beauty and Comanche were not stallions. They were good geldings trained to act as stallions for a movie role.

A young friend of mine was leading a young stallion on a loose line behind her after a grooming class in a show. She had raised this animal from a baby and knew him well. He was calmly following as he had always done. As they passed a gas-powered generator, someone turned it on. The unfamiliar noise startled the young horse and he reared knocking the girl face down. He kept rearing up and coming down on the middle of her back. She suffered a spinal cord injury and was paralyzed from the chest down. She lived in a wheelchair for about three years and then died due to poor circulation and an infection. Of course any horse would have become frightened, regardless of the sex of the animal. A stallion, however, is more powerful and more likely to try to master the situation.

In another case, a friend of mine and my husband's, a reputable businessman, had the reputation of being a top horseman. He had an Albino stallion that he was keeping and training for a friend. He did a beautiful job of training him for riding in both English and Western. The stallion learned to perform many crowd-pleasing tricks. He would bow, kneel in prayer, carry articles, skip, pull a quilt over himself and lie down and many more. I was appalled to learn this man was cruel in his training methods. Instead of taking time and being patient so that the horse would feel confident and willing, he was forced and rushed to gain quick results. The horse was smart. He developed a hatred for humans and would just be patient to catch the careless or unsuspecting. He would bite, rear up and fight and crowd. The horse would obey as long as this one man was handling him. He performed so well that adults and children wanted to get near and pet him, which was dangerous. Finally the man's wife insisted that the horse be gelded, but it was too late. He had developed fighting habits.

A truly good stallion was ruined by impatient, rushed training. The same could apply to a mare or a gelding. Investigate the trainer for safety's sake.

I don't pretend to be the best, but I do take time to train humanely and well.

Animals may not mean to hurt a human, but sudden, unexpected movements or unfamiliar noises can cause them to react out of self defense and fear. The first instinct is to get away and run. If they can't, they may try to fight. Stay calm, talk quietly and soothingly. Be firm, but kind. The bigger and stronger the animal, coupled with fear, can be difficult to control.

If you are upset, yell, scold, hit or jerk the animal around, it makes the situation worse, even dangerous.

When ready to buy, you might find a horse or pony in a classified ad. Beware. Have a veterinarian give a physical. A friend may know of an honest individual who is selling an animal because their children are no longer interested or they are moving and can't take the animal. Again, take the time and pay to have it checked. Beware of auctions where people are trying to get ride of undesirable animals. Check it out. I can't stress that enough.

In rare cases a riding school may have an animal that will be a good mount, but doesn't work well in a school. Be careful of school horses that have developed hard mouths or dead sides. The spirit may have been broken so that the animal is a "dog" and not suitable.

I keep urging; whatever you find, have a capable, trustworthy person help you select and then have a veterinarian check it out.

There are a few things you can do. Make sure the animal will lead easily without pulling or climbing up your back and will tie for grooming. Rub all over the back, underside, neck and ears to make sure he doesn't flinch as if he's been mistreated. Lift up the feet and check to make sure he'll cooperate.

One important reason you need a veterinarian to check, is that sometimes a less than honest person will drug the animal and the next day, after the drug has worn off, you'll have a shock. The sheath of the male and the teats of the mare need to be washed often. Be sure they don't mind being handled on their private parts.

Does he load in a trailer and travel well? Will he walk near or work with other horses without biting or kicking? If he has been run too much, and "cowboyed", he may become sour and uncooperative. By cowboyed I mean the horse that has been run to death in timed event classes without proper training, jerked around and hip hoorayed until he is an emotional wreck.

As a show judge I'm not against timed event classes. I find sadly about only two people out of ten know how to cue their horses properly.

And sadly not every horse has the physical build for what is ask of him.

Look at the set of his eyes. Are the eyes large, alert and set well apart? Are they set too close together or are the eyes very small? These are called "pig eyes".

A normal horse has good eyesight for a considerable distance. He can also see on both sides of him and well to the rear, BUT NOT DIRECTLY BEHIND HIM. Always let a horse know when you're going to be behind him or working with his tail (braiding). If he isn't aware you're there, he might panic and spook. This could mean a bad injury to you if he kicks, or he could rear and hurt himself.

If you purchase the horse and take him with you before a veterinarian checks, have a written agreement that the sale will be contingent upon a veterinarian's examination.

Ask to see the animal's medical records. Are his shots current, has he had a recent medical check-up, has the farrier been at work recently?

Check carefully on registration and breed papers. I have known of one horse to be sold on another horse's papers if their marks are identical or close enough. If you intend to breed or show in recognized shows, you want to be positive that you're getting honest papers.

As soon as the horse is all yours, take pictures from all sides and make a record of all marking, scars or anything of identification, such as brands or permanent injury scars. Keep the bill of sale with these pictures and papers. In the event the horse is stolen, you'll be able to give an accurate description of him.

This is a personal experience story from which I gained a hard, valuable lesson. Please read and heed.

Sometimes one may be offered the use of a horse in exchange for feeding and caring for him. It sounds good and one may think this is a great answer to their wishes. Remember, a friend today may not be a friend tomorrow. Have everything in writing and signed by ALL parties concerned.

A lady, from whom I was taking jumping lessons, became a close friend. She had an aged seventeen two hand Cleveland Bay hunter on which I had been practicing. She felt he was too old at twenty-seven to continue as a school horse, so she offered him to me, free of charge. He had been hunted for seventeen years by the Hunt Master and now as a school horse. He was too spirited and willing to just turn him out to pasture. She knew I loved him dearly and would take good care of him.

I wanted him badly but was already paying board on two other horses and felt I could not afford it. There was a teenage girl taking lessons from me whom I had treated like my own daughter. I had taken her on trips, to horse shows, out to lunch and so forth. I asked if I could talk to the girl's father and ask them to pay for his keep if I kept him with my horses. The owner was willing. I brought the girl and her father to talk to the owner and we reached an agreement, but nothing was in writing. After all, weren't these friends of mine?

This arrangement went on for a year. The girl had successfully shown the aged horse earning many blue ribbons and a few trophies. I finally found a hundred acres with a good block stable that I could lease for a reasonable price. I made arrangements to move the three horses, but the woman with whom I had been boarding did not feel good about me leaving. The girl came to me and said she and her father had talked to the horse's owner and had been given permission to keep on with the horse as they had. He was so willing that I was afraid he would be overworked, but I did not question the girl and the woman who owned the property we were on. Again, weren't we friends?

A few weeks later the owner called to chat and asked how the old boy was doing. I was stunned and told her what had happened. She was furious and screamed out that I was not to be trusted. I went to check on the horse and discovered that the girl and the property owner had given (or sold) the horse to a lady. They said she was handicapped and they were two old cripples together and laughed about it.

I went to talk to the lady and tell her that the horse was not theirs to give, but I was ordered off the property and treated like a criminal. I called the owner and told her. She took a deputy sheriff with her to straighten out the mess. It was a tragic experience and caused a lot of hard feelings that never should have happened. I still can't get over being lied to.

This brave old horse was put out of his misery at the age of thirty-two with arthritis and painful joints. I shed tears because he returned any love that was given to him. I had a twenty-five-year-old Morgan mare that was so willing to work and loved in return. She and this old horse became buddies. I called them the senior citizens of the pasture. I had purchased this mare at seventeen when she was retired from a cattle ranch in Nebraska, and used her to teach my husband to ride. I always kept my horses to a ripe old age and grieved over each and every one.

If you take a horse under such an arrangement, keep a written statement from all persons involved with a veterinarian record so that you will not be blamed for a previous illness or injury.

Now that you have your horse, you must start your own medical and stable records even if you're just pleasure riding and don't care about showing.

For the first five days, take your horse's temperature in both the A.M. and the P.M. Note the heart rate, pulse rate and any medical facts. Take these before and after exercises or training. Write down any remarks concerning general health such as alertness of eye, condition of coat, how he's standing, attitude and feeding habits. This will give you an excellent guide as to what is normal for your horse and will serve as a guide for future concerns.

This may sound like a lot of time and trouble and nonsense at first, but if your horse gets sick, is stolen or injured in some way, you can compare everything to the normal record.

CHARTS

Following is one example of how you might want to set your records. They're your records, so make them clear and understandable to you.

NAME Cherokee Challenge
SEX Gelding
BREED Thoroughbred/quarter
REGISTRATION NUMBER A4506321
DATE OF PURCHASE Jul-01-1979
SIRE Top Deck
DAM Miss Night Bar
PURCHASE PRICE $5,000.00
HEIGHT 15,3
WEIGHT 1100 LBS
FOALING DATE April-1977
COLOR Chestnut
MARKINGS star and blaze down over right nostril, both back feet white, blonde - red mane and tail

Date	Time	Temp.	Heart	Pulse	Remarks
7/1	8 AM	101.3	70	37	first day in new place
7/1	6 PM	101.7	68	35	seems good
7/2	8 AM	101.6	70	35	still eating well
7/2	6 PM	101.8	75	40	listless
7/3	8 AM	102.1	80	42	eyes tired looking not eating - called Vet.

****

			Cherokee	
Date	Time	Farrier	Vet.	Remark
7/3	9 AM		Dr. Know-It	Shipping Fever $110 shots & meds
7/5	4 PM		Dr Know-It	$25 checked OK
7/7	2 PM	Pete Jones		$140 trimmed & shod

****

STABLE PURCHASE RECORD

7/1	2 Ton hay $2,249.10
7/1	feeding tub & water bucket $ 68.00
7/1	grooming supplies $160.00
7/3	blanket & leg wraps $ 175.65

****

This is where I held my breath. I used to pay ninety cents for an eighty-five pound bale of hay. Now it's $24.99 for one bale of good hay or is $12.49 for plain pasture grass. A fifty pound bag of plain feed is now $15.00. More for a sick or aged animal.

A farrier charges $100 just for basic work. Corrective shoeing can go as high as $300. A basic veterinarian visit is around $85 to $100.

Boarding is understandably expensive. For full board you'll now pay anywhere from $600 to $1,000 per month, depending upon the value of the horse and what you expect the owners to do to help you. This is why I say it's easy to buy a horse, but the maintenance and equipment can cost a great deal. Know that whatever you do, it's going to cost a lot of money. Therefore, you not only will want to care properly for your animal because he's a living being with feelings, but you certainly don't want to waste money.

IMPORTANT FACTS

TEMPERATURE

Normal internal temperature of an adult horse is 99 to 101 degrees Fahrenheit. A foal can have 101.5 with nothing wrong. The temperature will change according to the type of work done, food eaten, weather changes or even illness. This is why it is important to keep a record for one week so that you may know what is normal for your horse and can be alerted if there is an abrupt or drastic change.

Buy a thermometer especially made to be used on equines. Tie a strong cord through the small hole on the end. If you do not have a tie, an upset horse can tighten the muscles around the rectum and pull the thermometer inside. Then you will need a veterinarian.

Before you insert the thermometer, place a tiny bit of plain Vaseline on your finger and rub it over the thermometer to make it easier and more pleasant for the animal. After using, wash thoroughly in cool to warm water with Ivory soap, rinsing well. Before using it again, rinse it in tap water and shake it down. I wrap mine in gauze and place it back in the box.

If you use the thermometer often without sterilization, or on several animals, infections and minute parasites can be spread.

To insert the thermometer, pat the horse on the rump and speak soothingly. Pull the tail to one side and hold it there. Gently insert the thermometer against one side and not in the center. In the center you are more likely to just get the temperature of the feces. Leave it in for 3 to 5 minutes. Don't forget to clean it and place it in a safe place. Keep your records current.

The normal temperature may be slightly higher in the PM. To check for external temperature, feel the part of the body in question. If it feels warmer than usual, first aid may be required.

It is important that you run your hand over your horse daily, especially if they're in the pasture. Observe the alertness of eyes and check for bruises or injuries. If there is a cut or puncture wound, you can treat it more effectively by finding it in time.

I know I'm repeating some things over and over, but they are important to remember. Your horse is going to be healthier, safer to be around and more willing to work with you if he is feeling good and trusts you. I don't advise going to pieces over every little thing, but you can prevent a more serious situation by keeping "on the ball". If in doubt, consult your vet.

Treat your horse as you would a human baby. Neither one can talk and tell you about their aches and pains, so you have to use common sense and take care of them.

PULSE

Although the average pulse of the horse at rest is 36 to 40 beats per minute, the following can be normal. That's why it's important to keep your own horse's readings.

AT REST
Full Grown Stallion	28 to 32
Mare	34 to 40
Mare in Foal	36 to 43
Gelding	33 to 38
Foal up to 6 weeks	70 to 90
6 months to 1 year	45 to 60
Up to 3 years for Cold or Filly	40 to 50

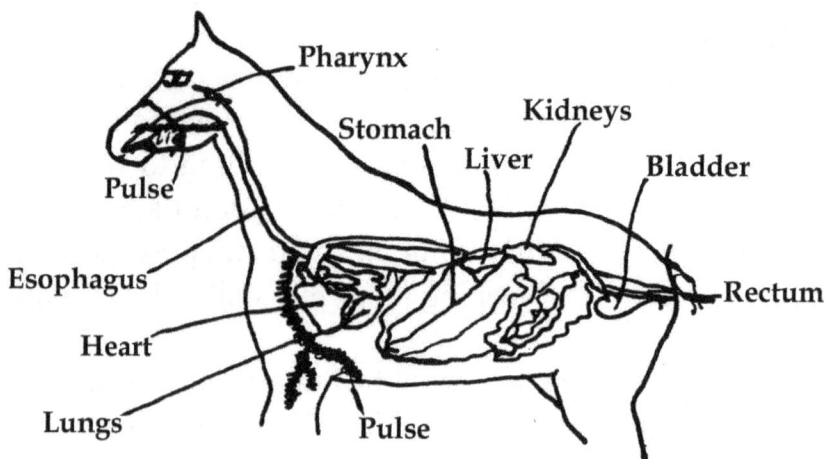

The pulse can be counted where a large artery is close to the skin and over a hard tissue. The easiest place is the jaw. In front of the heavy muscle in the cheek, an artery runs from the jaw, around the lower part of the jawbone and up the outside of the jawbone to the face. Another good point is the artery inside the front leg about even with the elbow.

<u>HEART</u>

The heart is located near the sixth rib about level with the elbow and in line with the shoulder. Check before and after exercise.

Normal count can be 60 to 80 at rest. It is easier to check on the left side by lifting and gently pulling the leg forward so the spot for the heart can be located. Know what is normal for your horse.

While I was attending a race over timbers, I watched a group of horses drawing near the finish line where I was standing. As the horses came across the line, the horse in front staggered, fell heavily on his side and slid to stop right in front of me. I could see he was dead. It was determined the six-year-old had suffered a heart attack. That poor baby must have been in pain for a long time, but kept on to please his rider. An animal does not have to be old to have heart problems. A vet check prior to the race might not have discovered the weak heart.

Strong exercise without rest over a period of time is hard on the heart. Several days of rest and then strong exercise without gradually building to it is dangerous. Working too hard soon after eating or drinking a lot of water can be a problem.

LUNGS

The air that is exhaled should be about the same as the body temperature. It should have considerable moisture and leave each nostril with the same force. There should not be any strong or unpleasant odor. The normal respiratory rate for a horse at rest is 8 to 16 per minute. Both nostrils should be open and clean. (I dip a cloth is cool water and gently wipe out the nostrils each day.) The respiratory rate will be faster in a frightened animal, very young ones, after exercise, after eating, if pregnant and possibly if the weather is hot and humid.

If you are suspicious about the respiratory rate, keep the animal quiet while observing him over a one to two hour period. If there is still a suspicious rate, then call the veterinarian. If there is a continuous discharge from the nostrils, call the veterinarian. Better a veterinarian bill, or to be laughed at, than a sick or dead animal.

If the animal is coughing, observe him for at least an hour. He may be having trouble swallowing something. If the cough continues, call the veterinarian.

HEAVES

In a respiratory disease, this starts by difficulty in breathing, a dry, wheezing cough, and, if allowed to go without treatment, the stomach will enlarge. The flanks will fall away and the horse will develop emphysema. This can, in rare cases, be inherited. Most of the time it is due to poor care on the part of the human. It can come about by feeding dusty, poor quality hay, dusty feed, having a poorly ventilated or dirty stable and lots of cobwebs and dust. The condition is not curable, but it can be helped. Once an animal has had a serious illness of heaves, that animal should NEVER be required to run, jump or work for the rest of his life. He can be gently and quietly ridden on short trail rides with lots of rest stops. Never work him until he is out of breath; it won't take long for that to happen. He must be given the very best of hay and feed and must have fresh water at all times. A little water sprinkled on the hay or really warm water mixed with the feed is a big help to a sick or even a well horse. Please don't be cruel enough to sell him to someone without telling the truth about his condition.

A horse with heaves will be in extreme pain and have a fever. He will be reluctant to move. If forced to move, there will be a stumbling, rambling gait and trembling. In advanced cases, the horse should be placed on high quality pasture with fresh water and not required to work at all for several months. If there is no improvement, then be kind and retire him and love him for the rest of his days. If this is a financial hardship, then have him humanely put to sleep. I beg of you again, do not sell him or give him to someone who will not care for him properly. They serve us and love us unconditionally. We must do the same for them.

STOMACH

A horse's stomach is small in comparison to the size of his body. The stomach empties about 5 or 6 hours after eating. After that the horse weakens rapidly until fed again. Avoid hard work or exercise right after eating.

Keep the feeding schedule as regular as possible. The best schedule is three times a day, although twice is acceptable. Determine, with the help of your veterinarian, how much hay, feed or vitamins that particular horse should get in a day. The feeding will vary according to the size of the animal and the type of work required.

When I had a riding school, I fed around 6 AM. While the horses were eating hay, we cleaned stalls and filled water buckets. They then received grain while we checked tack and got supplies ready for the day. Horses were groomed and by 8 AM were ready for the first lesson. I gave one and a half hours of rest while the aides rested, studied or did some assigned work. They did not work at noon for an hour and were given a small amount of grain. By 6 PM the horses were fed again and not used until 7:30 for one last lesson. No horse was worked all day. The ones worked in the morning had the evening off. The ones worked in the afternoon had the following morning off. Some were worked morning and evening, but not afternoon. It depended upon their age, temperament, weather and students.

I know some people laughed at me for being so careful with the animals, but the horses were willing and safe to work with, and all of mine lived to a ripe old age in comfort.

At night they were either turned out into the field or to a stall with fresh water and clean, fresh straw on the floor. We all had Monday off.

Since the student instructors were volunteers, I would allow them to swim the horses, bareback, in the pond. Horses and people loved it. I also gave free riding lessons to the volunteers.

If a horse had happened to be worked hard, such as in a long jumping session, I only gave him a pint of water and half a flake of hay until he rested a short time. Then he was given the remainder of his feed. Never feed or water an animal that is just getting over a fright or unusual excitement.

It is a good practice to feed bran mash once a week to horses that are worked or in the pasture regularly. Every Saturday, with the regular feed, I gave two cups of bran, two cups of mineral oil and four cups of hot water. This will vary according to the size, age and health condition of the animal. Again, consult your veterinarian. The vet would far rather be consulted than have to rush out and try to save an animal.

Bran mash is recommended by a majority of veterinarians for any stomach upset or bowel problem. Some add chopped apples, carrots, or anything the animal likes to eat. The bran is important to animals out in the open field, or those with very little grazing, because they can ingest a lot of sand or dirt which causes stomach problems.

<u>COLIC</u>

Colic is a dangerous sickness that occurs in all horses of all ages (just as in small children). Most cases can be helped. It can be caused by overloading the stomach, cooling the horse off too quickly after a workout, giving too much water to drink while he is still hot, standing him sweaty and tired in a stall without a proper cool down or even a digestive problem.

A horse with colic will look frequently at his flanks because he is in pain and uncomfortable. He may bite at his sides and lie down refusing to get up. He may be in such pain as to start kicking and rolling, throwing himself around. He can get caste (or stuck) and be unable to move. Force him to stay on his feet and slowly walk him to try to ease the pain. Call for help immediately.

If he is allowed to roll and throw himself around, he is in danger of rupturing the stomach, bursting his diaphragm or twisting his intestines, resulting in a painful death.

Again, a personal experience: When I first started in the horse business and was boarding, the people had a valuable, registered two-year-old colt. One evening he had signs of colic. We walked him and did all that was required, but nothing helped. Finally they agreed to call the veterinarian. He gave the horse a shot, gave us medicine to put in his water and left us to continue walking him. This went on most of the night. He died before dawn in spite of all we did. An autopsy showed bailing twin had been taken into the stomach and had twisted around his intestines. A horse cannot vomit or cough up anything in his throat.

A careless person had left the twine in his hay. This is why I insist that all twine, cords, papers, and everything be picked up at all times. Hay is checked carefully before feeding to make sure nothing is in it that can harm an animal.

One morning I grabbed a double arm load of hay to feed another young, valuable stallion in an outside paddock. He snorted, backed and refused to come near it to eat. I dropped it and out crawled a harmless black snake that was about four feet long. I had carried that snake out in the hay. Do check your hay. Be careful that it is dry and of good quality.

Another case had a happy ending. After school one evening, I found that there had been a fight between Cherokee and a Palomino, Meloso D'Oro, that had come from Arthur Godfrey. (I learned later the Palomino was a ridgling or proud cut, meaning someone had tried to castrate him and botched the job. He could no longer breed, but still had the desire. It drove him crazy.)

Cherokee had a broken jaw that had to be wired, and torn flesh that had to be stitched. He had to be hand fed small amounts several times a day. I was teaching public school at the time, so a friend volunteered to feed him during the day for me. He also had to be given a shot in the muscle in his neck twice a day.

I had been giving him water through a small tube, but apparently it wasn't enough. About eight days later my husband and I came in from work and went straight to the stable. We found Cherokee on the floor rolling his eyes and groaning. My friend, who had been helping me, walked in a few seconds later. I had forced the horse to stand and was walking him. I called the vet, but he was on call clear across the county which meant he couldn't get there any time soon.

My husband went to get some Milk of Magnesia. My friend stood on a bucket and poured it in Cherokee's mouth. I think more got on us and than in him. I sent my husband home to get our hot water bottle with the enema tube and two five gallon containers of hot water. The water was just very warm by the time we got it. That sweet horse stood while I poured water into his rectum, refilling the bottle and starting again.

We walked him more and he began to eliminate a small amount of colored water. At 10 PM, by the time the vet arrived, Cherokee had had a good bowel movement and relieved himself. The doctor gave him a shot and he was doing well.

If you need to keep a clean tube to get water down a horse, please be sure you know what you're doing. The tube could easily go down into the lung area and kill the horse.

This is an excellent reason why your horses should be checked daily. The proper treatment given in time can mean the difference between death and quality life for your animal.

KIDNEYS

As can be seen in the drawing on page 25, the kidneys are located where the weight of the saddle is on them. An ill-fitting saddle, or riding double, can cause pain to the horse's kidneys.

Organic diseases of the kidneys of the horse are rare. It is very serious when it does occur though. Consult your veterinarian.

If your animal is showing signs of having trouble urinating, it could be kidney stones or an infection. The horse may show a squatting position and strain while trying to urinate. Older horses can have kidney problems due to age and wear and tear.

Feed a bran mash with some salt so that the horse will drink water. The veterinarian can give a shot to act as a diuretic along with other medication. Loads of fresh water is vitally important. (For humans, too.)

Musty or dry, bad hay can cause Polyuria. With this there will be a heavy discharge that is slightly colored. The horse might have eaten dirt, sand or dust and drank so much water that he makes himself sick. If this is not treated, the horse will lose weight and slowly die.

Avoid high protein hay and feeds.

If there is stiffness in the rear legs, signs of pain when you press the loins, or if there is a rolling gait and general discomfort, this could be Nephritis (infection). The pulse increases and the temperature rises. As the disease progresses, there could be skin eruptions. Unless a veterinarian treats the horse, he will have to be destroyed.

Until the vet arrives, keep the horse steaming warm. Give a wet mash and place a hot blanket over the loins. If the legs are stiff and show signs of pain, wrap bandages (not tightly) around the legs and keep him warm. Be careful you don't cut off circulation.

If there is a sign of blood in the urine, this might be a serious strain or injury. The strain could come from an ill-fitted saddle, too much weight over the kidneys, rolling on a rocky surface, or an infection. Sometimes too much fresh, rich grass with a lot of sweet clover can contribute to this. There could be signs of stiffness and soreness. Know your horse and be alert. Give plenty of fresh water. Keep the horse warm and quiet. Most importantly, call the veterinarian.

INTESTINES

Problems can be from an infection, parasites (such as bots) or a mixture of dry food and heavy grass. This can cause constipation. If not treated, this can lead to colic, twisted intestines or more serious problems.

Parasites cause a great deal of pain and often impacted bowels (constipation). Sometimes there might be diarrhea off and on. A slight yellowish texture can be seen in the mucous membranes and the breath will have a foul odor.

Give laxatives as recommended by your vet. Enemas are useful, IF YOU KNOW HOW TO GIVE THEM. If you don't, you could cause severe pain or even rupture the intestines.

About every hour give one quart of water. The stomach and intestines are already swollen and painful. Do not continue to load them with water or food until the condition is cured. Walk the horse a little. Keep him quiet and in quiet surroundings while avoiding chilling him. Twisted intestines can be caused by violent rolling, sudden falls or slips, parasites, swallowing string or any foreign object.

The horse will make crouching motions but will hesitate to lie down. He might even try to sit on his haunches like a dog. He becomes dull and listless. The pulse is weak, then rapid, then weak again. The respiration is short and labored. The temperature may soar and there will be straining of the bowels. Again keep him warm, quiet and free of drafts or chills. Treat as for colic and call the veterinarian.

Diarrhea in foals may be from a nursing mare that has not been fed properly. It could also be caused by the mare coming in season, or it could be an infection.

A veterinarian will prescribe the appropriate medication to be given. Wash the foal's rump and legs (whatever has been touched by the discharge) with warm water and Ivory soap. Rinse well with warm water and dry thoroughly. Keep him clean. Keep him warm and dry or otherwise skin burns can result and be very uncomfortable

FEET

No feet, no horse. Meaning that if the feet are bad under the body weight, the horse cannot be used. If not corrected and treated properly, the horse will likely need to be destroyed.

The hoof is a horn-like substance covering tissues, bones, nerves and blood vessels. It needs to be kept sound and healthy and trimmed on a regular basis.

All parts of the hoof grow downward at the rate of about a third of an inch per month. It takes approximately a year for the average hoof to grow down completely from the time the horn grows from the coronary band to the point where the hoof is trimmed.

There is no more pain involved in cutting a hoof than there is in cutting one's fingernails. If a cut or a puncture is made into the nerves and blood vessels of the hoof, this could cause the same pain as a person tearing a fingernail to the quick.

The soft ridge at the top of the hoof is the coronary band. From this point the horn-like substance starts to grow out and down. The surface of the hoof is similar to a thin varnish called the periople. The periople acts as a protective coating to keep moisture in the proper places and helps ensure a good growth rate.

The hoof wall carries the majority of the horse's weight and protects the soft areas inside the hoof. The bars give strength and act as a brace and as a hinge. The sole covers the ground surface of the hoof. It helps protect against hard or painful objects. The sole also protects the soft, sensitive tissue inside the hoof. Its concave structure helps the foot grip the ground properly.

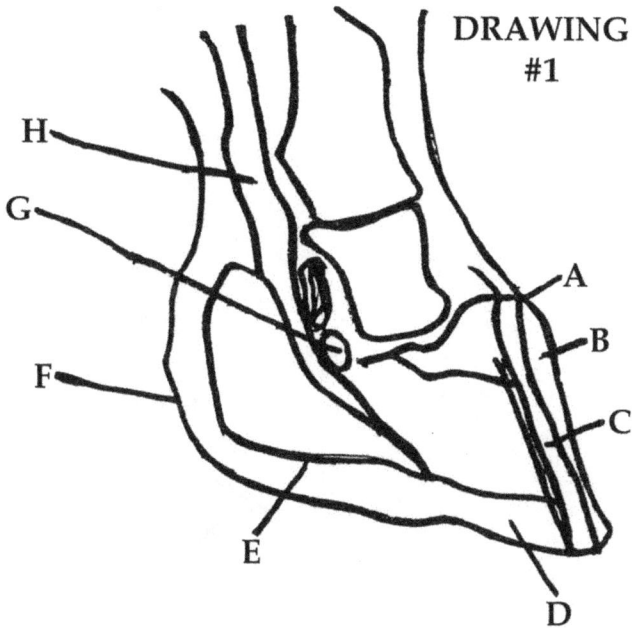

DRAWING #1

Drawing #1

A   Coronary band
B   Wall
C   Laminae
D   Sole
E   Frog
F   Heel
G   Navicular Bone
H   Deep digital flexor tendon

**DRAWING
#2**

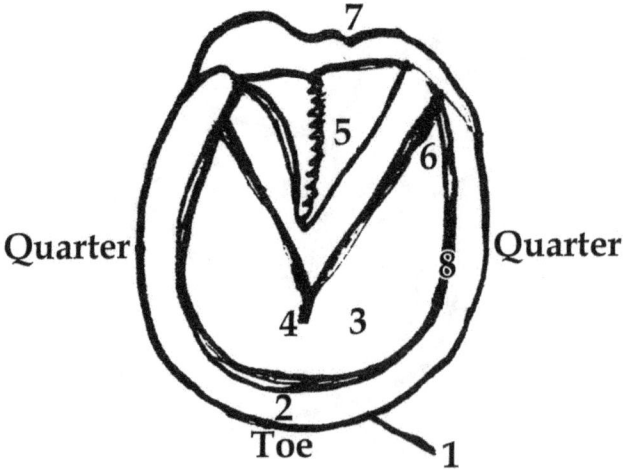

Drawing # 2

1. Periople
2. Wall
3. Sole
4. Apex of frog
5. Center of frog
6. Bar
7. Bulb of the heel
8. Line between wall

The frog is the triangular-shaped part toward the back of the hoof. Its purpose is to soften shocks and jars to the foot and to help the foot get a better grip when in motion. The frog also helps the horse to "brake" without slipping. Its touch and release motion helps the blood to circulate through the foot and leg. The frog must be kept soft without being mushy soft. The area around the frog must be kept cleaned out and in proper condition.

Even if a hoof is not shod (wearing shoes), it absolutely must be trimmed regularly. This should be done by a qualified farrier. A qualified farrier will have attended a training school that teaches about bones, muscles, nerves and blood vessels as well as diseases of the foot. He also will know how to observe the way a horse walks and carries his weight in the event he needs to do corrective shoeing. Ensure that the farrier is well known and has an excellent reputation according to his work. He should be known for doing the work well and correctly, and for keeping the appointments.

The hoof should be cleaned and checked daily whether the horse is used or not. It is vitally important to clean the hoof before and after working or exercising. A good hoof ointment should be used in dry weather or on dry ground. Ask the farrier what is best for your animal.

Never use a hoof ointment that has grease, petroleum or lanolin in it. A greasy hoof will not absorb moisture and the hoof becomes very dry. This retards healthy growth, causes cracks in the hoof and can cause serious problems.

Trimming of the hoof should begin at just a few months of age. This not only encourages healthy growth but can be used in correcting minor leg deformities. It will help the horse move correctly and be well-balanced.

I usually start a three-day-old by rubbing them all over with a cloth, gently lifting the hoof and tapping on it with a finger and showing the baby that he, or she, can be handled without fear or pain. If they seem unsure, I let them lean against their dam while I handle them. In rare cases the mare might not cooperate. Don't force it, but don't give up on it either.

Have you ever tried walking in a shoe that has a slightly higher heel than the other one or shoes that have worn down on one side and throw you off balance? Sure you can move, but if you walked for several days with these shoes you would have backaches, hip problems, pulled muscles and many discomforts. If you had to carry a weight in addition to your own with uncomfortable, ill-fitting shoes, you would understand the discomfort of the horse and take better care of him.

Under three years of age the hoof is still developing. It should be trimmed, cleaned and taken care of, but not necessarily shod unless you are trying to train for some special event. If you are going to be walking the horse on a hard surface (such as the street) ask the farrier for a special shoe, or coating, to keep the horse from slipping or causing his legs and hip to be strained.

If a horse is left standing in a stall, his feet will need attention more often. One excellent way to help a pastured horse, or an outside horse, is to dampen the ground around the water tub.

If a horse stands in manure or urine (soaked bedding), the periople will be destroyed which can cause lameness and pain in the leg and hip. Do not file the outer surface of the hoof or use any abrasive material that would damage or destroy the hoof. Too much moisture causes rot to occur on the frog which cripples the horse.

When being shod, make sure the nails are driven in low or they could damage and cause pain to the hoof. Be sure the shoe has been fitted to the hoof and not the hoof to the shoe. Shoes should not be left on longer than necessary. Even when they seem to fit well they could be too tight and cause the hoof to grow out of proportion which throws the horse off balance. If the shoe is left on too long they wear thin and the nails shift causing tears in the hoof wall. If a horse loses a shoe, do not ride or work him until the shoe is reset. Do not attempt the job yourself.

If the shoe has been violently pulled loose, or caused to shift, there will be damage to the hoof. Take safety precautions until the farrier can work on him. Have pads of gause or thick cotton padding, two large pieces of white cloth (preferably cotton cloth about eighteen inches wide), medical tape and regular leg wrap. Place the padding around the affected area that is damaged and stand the hoof on one of the clean, white cloths. Wrap the cloth around the hoof carefully. Use the second cloth and wrap this up allowing some to go a short distance onto the leg.

Leave a very small amount of slack for free movement of the hoof and leg and to make sure circulation is not cut. Tape the cloths securely in place around the foot. Start the leg wrap around the hoof and up the leg to hold all bandaging in place. Don't wrap so tight you cut circulation. When placing a leg wrap on, twist it every now and then so that it will lie flat and stay in place.

PLEASE NOTE: If there is a wound, clean with warm water and Ivory liquid soap and carefully rinse well with warm water. Do not place a heavy ointment on any wound because the farrier, or the veterinarian, will have trouble seeing the actual damage or wound. Keep a written record of everything you have done so that anyone who handles the horse will be informed of the care. You might not be available when the farrier or veterinarian arrives and they will need to know what has been done.

If the wound is deep, keep it open so that proper drainage can occur and healing will be from the inside out. If it heals on the outside before the inside, problems will continue and will get worse.

Bruises and injuries to the foot are common due to rough or rocky ground, too dry or too moist conditions, poor shoeing or going too long without proper care of the hoof and shoes. Daily observation helps you know whether your horse is showing signs of lameness or painful movements in the hip or stifle area.

Conformation faults such as pigeon-toed, splay-footed, winging or paddling and such type of poor conformation can be helped with corrective shoeing.

A young horse can be damaged for life in tendons, bones, muscles or ligaments if the feet are neglected or shod incorrectly. Young horses running in pasture or standing in an enclosed area for a period of time can cause a flare or spreading of the hoof. This causes a harmful leverage on the leg and hip or shoulder. This has to be corrected gradually.

HOOF PROBLEMS

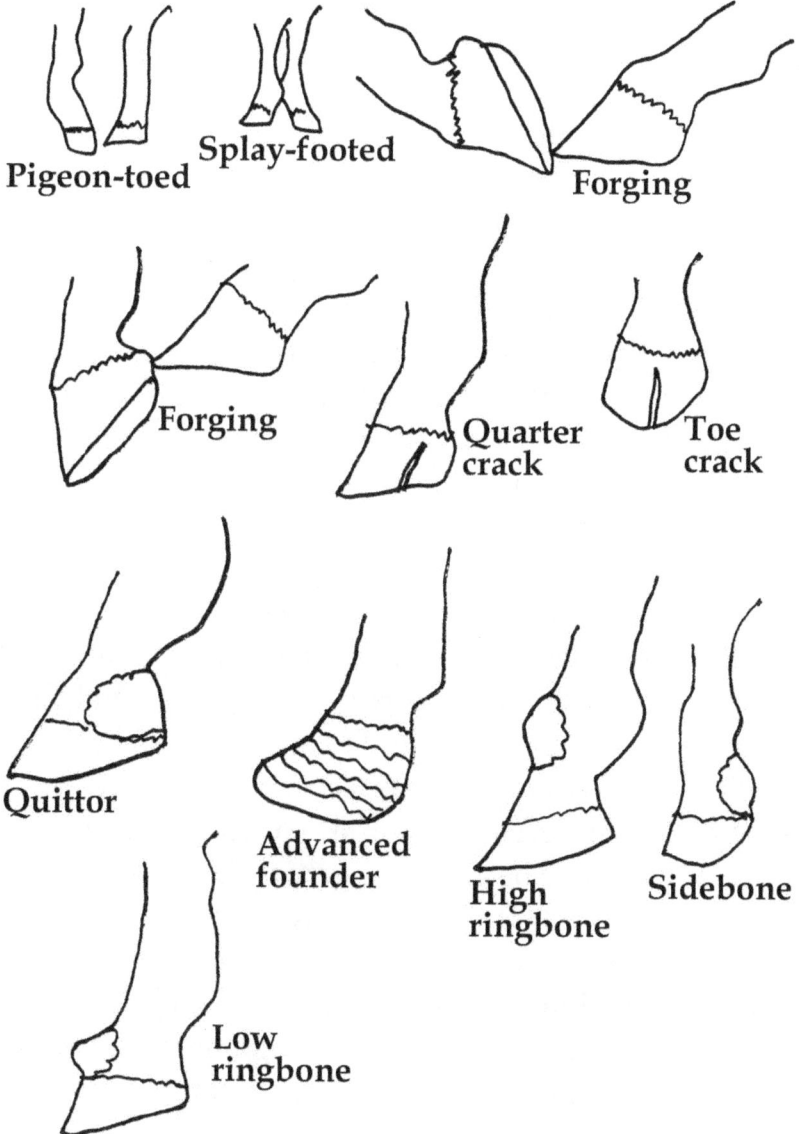

Pigeon-toed

Splay-footed

Forging

Forging

Quarter crack

Toe crack

Quittor

Advanced founder

High ringbone

Sidebone

Low ringbone

PIGEON-TOED or turned in, means the toes are turned toward each other which throws the animal off balance. This can be helped if the inside of the hoof is trimmed down all the way from the toe to the heel. This helps force the foot to turn out more. Don't trim too much at once, and most importantly, don't allow too much time between trimmings.

SPLAY-FOOTED or turned too far out, can be helped by trimming the outside of the hoof down. Exercising a horse too young, constantly in a circle on a lunge line can cause some of the problems. Up to one year of age, the horse should only be asked to walk, stand, back a little, come along or work in extra large circles. Walking over poles laid flat on the ground can help, but don't ask too much of the one-year-old. Concentrate on allowing to be handled all over, obeying voice commands and standing straight.

As I've said before, I lift a little one's foot and gently tap on the bottom to get him used to being handled. The farrier will need to trim properly, but not shoe. At two years of age I lay across the back for a few minutes, or, according to the breed and size of the animal, may tie a fifty pound sack of feed on the back to prepare him for carrying weight.

Well into the twos I get him accustomed to feeling a bit in his mouth, but do not pull on it. Nearing three I use two long lines and walk behind him getting him accustomed to being directed by the pull of the reins and bit. By three mine are ready to be mounted and guided. It is a rare occasion that I have a horse fight me or get frightened by my lengthy training. Yes, I take longer than some trainers, but mine are never afraid and are willing to please because they haven't been hurt or frightened. Also, mine stay healthy until a ripe old age.

Most Thoroughbred trainers will mount an older one-year-old and train them for the tracks. These horses break down quickly, meaning their health is shot and they're damaged or hurt easily. Their poor little backs have not fully developed at this age.

FORGING OR OVERREACHING means that the back feet are moving too far forward too soon and hitting the heels of the front feet.

Hitting often can cause a painful bruise and a raw area. If the overreach is extreme, it can cause an injury to the fetlock. To help correct this, the farrier can shorten the heel of the front shoe and shorten the toe of the hind shoe. The heel of the front shoe is raised slightly and the heel of the back shoe is lowered slightly. Some people place balls (rubber rings) on the feet to help prevent injuries such as these. If the heel or the fetlock of the front foot has been injured, keep it clean and free of dirt. Clean the hair, dirt and scabs from the infected area. Clean with warm water and a mild soap and use a lanolin-based ointment to keep out flies, bugs, germs and anything that would prevent healing.

CROSS-FIRING means that a rear foot is reaching forward to strike the diagonal front foot. For instance the left hind foot might strike the right front foot. A special shoe is required, but treat the wounds as you would a foraging stride. If the hoof, especially the frog, becomes too hard and dry, stand that foot in a tub of warm water. If the problem has been allowed to progress too far, apply a soaked bandage and cover with a burlap bag. Tie carefully so as not to cut circulation.

If the frog is not supple enough to absorb the weight of the movements, this can cause a sore hip or shoulder. On the other hand, too much moisture can cause rot or other problems.

CORNS are usually caused by an injury to the wall or sole of the foot. A small blood vessel is usually ruptured causing soreness. The front feet are more likely to get corns because most of the weight is thrown to the front. The affected area must be cut out and drained and kept clean. Daily cleaning of the hoof is necessary to spot troubles.

QUARTER CRACKS (on the side of the hoof) and toe cracks can be caused by dryness, standing in stalls with poor flooring or too much work without proper trimming and shoeing. Sometimes the cracks are deep enough for blood and pus to ooze through. This is very painful to the horse. Keep the hoof clean, have corrective shoeing done and apply a good foot dressing to keep the hoof soft and pliable. Ask your farrier for advice.

QUITTOR is an injury that causes infection or inflammation inside the hoof. It could be caused by a severe bruise, a nail puncture, a wire or glass cut that has scabbed over or an infected corn. Often swelling will occur around the coronet, causing the horse to refuse to place any weight on the foot. Sometimes the pain is so great the horse will lie down and refuse to get up. To check for internal injuries, gently tap the hoof with a light weight metal tool. Most of the time the horse will jerk back or wince from the pain. The veterinarian will need to cut into the area and remove the infected tissue. Keep open for proper drainage and to heal from the inside out. Treat as a puncture wound. Bandage to keep out germs and dirt.

FOUNDER or LAMINITIS is usually found in the front feet but can occur in any foot. This is caused by a disturbance in the blood circulation since the hoof does not expand enough to allow for this. It can become very painful. Once founder occurs, it can happen again. There is no permanent cure.

Founder may occur due to: 1) bad feed; 2) overfeeding or drinking too much water especially immediately after working, after excitement; 3) cooling off too quickly after being hot; 4) constant work on hard ground; 5) being overweight; and 6) working too hard without proper preparation. For instance if the animal has been standing all week in a stall, or even in a pasture, and then taken out to run or jump, it is hard on the feet and the whole body. They must be walked until warmed up. I've seen people leave the horse in a stall all week, come out on the weekend, jump on him and urge him to immediately run a distance. Think how you would feel to be dragged out of bed from a sound sleep and forced to run a distance without training for it. Show care and compassion. Silly? Maybe, but better to go overboard taking care of him than to lose him to neglect.

Symptoms may be high temperature, fast or labored breathing, sweating, loss of appetite and peculiar standing.

Sometimes he will stand with the weight of his body on his back feet to avoid pressure on the front. If not treated, the muscles of the chest will waste away because of the poor standing. The shoe should be removed and the feet trimmed regularly. Be careful that the feet do not become bruised by standing on the wrong type of flooring or ground. Consult your veterinarian about the correct food for your particular horse. The horse must not be allowed to gain weight and MUST NOT be worked until approved by the veterinarian or the farrier. Start with light work on easy ground for a short period of time. Never allow this horse to be overheated, overfed or overtired. Cool off slowly and properly, being careful to check the food and water intake.

Temporary relief from pain might be to stand the foot in very warm water just past the fetlock for about an hour and then cool with slightly warm water. If the horse is unable to stand, then wrap the foot in cloths soaked in very warm water for about two weeks. Do this once in the morning and once in the evening unless the horse is in so much pain he might require the treatment more often. After the horse has improved, regular shoeing is imperative.

To avoid the possibility of foundering, make sure to supply GOOD QUALITY hay and feed. Again, consult your veterinarian. Protect the horse from drafts or cold air. (Have a good blanket for the winter.)

If he has been worked hard and is sweaty, take the time to walk him and cool him off slowly and thoroughly. When transporting, protect him from abrupt changes in temperature. If the legs are hosed off after working, make sure he is dry and cooled off properly before leaving him. If there has been a lot of exhaustion or excitement, allow the animal to remain quiet and free of drafts.

It's a little more expensive, but if the horse has trouble standing, there are special clinics that can place a canvas sling under his belly and hold him upright.

THRUSH is a disease that affects the frog and soft parts of the hoof. It is usually caused by unsanitary conditions. It can occur after the horse has stood, or worked, often in muddy or too moist conditions.

Standing in a dirty stall or walking where a lot of manure and urine has collected can cause thrush. A discharge or foul-smelling matter around the frog alerts you to the possibility of thrush. If allowed to go untreated, pus will appear and lameness will develop. The hoof and heel will be hot.

To treat this, a farrier, or veterinarian, should trim away the infected area being careful to avoid excessive bleeding. Clean the hoof thoroughly with warm water and mild soap. Apply medication around the frog. If the damage is severe, the foot would have to be bandaged to keep out dirt and harmful matter. This must be done daily until healing is evident. Continue to keep clean and apply the medication as long as the farrier or veterinarian recommends. Often a special pad is placed under the shoe to protect the affected part. Keep the stall, or standing area, free of filth and have a deep bedding to ensure comfort. Care should be taken to work easy and slowly until the hoof can move freely. Do not risk re-injury by working too soon or too hard.

CONTRACTED HEELS are caused by poor shoeing, too much time between shoeing jobs or excessive dry conditions of the hoof. This usually happens from faulty shoeing which causes a pinched heel. The frog is pinched and can't do its job. It might be caused by a disease or injury to the foot or even a conformation fault. It is painful but can be helped with corrective shoeing.

NAVICULAR is scary and should be. It occurs inside the hoof and often is not detected until it has eaten the inside of the hoof away. This usually occurs in the front feet and most of the time only one foot. It is heartbreaking because it can mean either putting the horse to sleep or pulling the nerve in the affected leg. When the nerves are pulled, the horse has no feeling and thus is entirely dependent on you to move him on safe, easy ground as he cannot feel anything. Additionally, the horse can be dangerous to ride because he may stumble or fall more easily.

Usually this is an inherited trait which affects the small navicular bone. More often this occurs in horses that are required to jump, landing heavily on the front feet. The faster or harder an animal has to move, the greater the weight proportion and shock to the front legs, such as timed events, jumping or racing. This disease comes on so slowly that it is difficult to detect without X-rays until it is almost too late.

An early sign may be the horse hesitates to stand long on the affected leg and shifts around without standing squarely. He may point the foot, but if both feet are affected he will shift constantly trying to relieve the pressure from the pain.

He will appear to be stiff when first worked and may dig a toe in the ground and stumble. The toe of the shoe will wear down quickly or, if unshod, the toe of the hoof will break and split. The horse might take short steps and even fall to his knees if asked to work. When backed he will set the affected foot down with care and then pass his weight quickly to another foot. This causes stiffness and lameness in the shoulder and hip joints because he is putting his weight in an unnatural position. In advanced cases, the horse will sweat, become tense and frustrated. The foot will be hot to the touch and he will flinch when pressure is applied around the hoof. The frog will often shrink and become infected.

Do not ask him to run and please be kind enough to not turn him loose with someone who will be careless with him. Unless you are willing to just love him and turn him loose in the pasture, it is kinder to put him down. Corrective shoeing will help temporarily, but his usefulness as a working animal is over.

SIDEBONE occurs more often in the front feet. It comes on slowly and is not as laming as most diseases. In its formation stage, the horse can be lame, but after the growth calcifies lameness disappears. In the meantime, do not work him much. Sidebone occurs when inflammation of the cartilage of the frog expands the frog and heel. It can also be caused by bruises and diseases of the foot.

You will first notice a slightly hard swelling on one or both sides of the hoof near the heel. The deposit of bony matter slowly develops for some time before the actual bony growth can be felt or seen. Usually the outside of the hoof is affected first. The horse will point the toe to relieve pressure. In severe cases, the affected area will bulge and be hard. When first taken from the stall, he may be stiff and sore but will loosen after <u>light</u> exercise. Apply bandages soaked in cold water to relieve the fever and keep the foot moist.

This is usually inherited, therefore horses with sidebone or navicular should never be bred. There is no need to pass on the heartbreaking traits to another animal.

<u>RINGBONE</u> is an unsoundness in the pastern, a rough, bony growth just above the edge of the hoof. If it occurs nearer the fetlock, it is called high ringbone. The low ringbone nearer the hoof causes more lameness. A more serious form involves the back tendon as well as the joint.

Symptoms may be that the horse places more pressure on the heel instead of the toe and the ankle area is rigid. If it occurs in the back feet, the toe will strike the ground first but the ankle area will be rigid. This, too, appears gradually. The horse needs rest. Keep the fever down and ask the farrier if special shoeing is needed. This cannot be cured and the animal will be useless. Either love him and turn him out to pasture or put him down.

There are many diseases and possible injuries of the feet due to the fact that they support all that body weight and touch the ground full of filth. Also, the blood has to work hard to circulate from the legs, through the foot area and back up. Anything that disturbs the normal flow of circulation can cause problems. No feet, no horse.

EYES

The whale and the horse have the largest eyes of any animal. Whereas a pupil in the human eye is round, the pupil in the horse's eye is horizontal. He can see on both sides, front and back, but not directly behind him. Due to the length of his face, he does have a blind spot immediately below his nose. This is why he puts his head down and sometimes turns his head to one side so that he can see under himself.

When he is young and green, or facing some strange object, you should let him walk up to it quietly and look closely so that he can satisfy himself that it's nothing scary. If you are facing new or unfamiliar jumps, he should be allowed to walk up to them first in order to judge the distance. Otherwise he depends entirely on your cues to him. He can only see so far in front, but you're up higher and can see farther, therefore it is your responsibility to stay alert and guide him.

The horse has three eyelids: two external ones and one which is a membrane, or a sheet of elastic cartilage. The third eyelid helps remove particles of dirt or foreign matter from the eye and helps keep the eyeball moist by spreading moisture. In extreme cases of injury or shock, this membrane is likely to close over the eye as nature's means of further protection.

The lacrimal gland secretes tears to keep the eye moist and free of foreign matter that would dry the eye or injure it. These tears will also flow if he has an allergy.

Again, a personal experience: Cherokee Challenge had allergies that showed up every Spring and Fall. The areas around his eyes filled with fluid and he shed tears constantly. There are shots that can be given in extreme cases. The best you can do is keep the face washed clean so that the skin is not irritated. Check with your veterinarian as to whether a good eyewash would be beneficial and how and when to use it.

In the average horse the white of the eye should be clear with no signs of blood vessels. In the older horse, the white might become yellowish.

In two cases it has been my experience to see horses actually cry in grief. In both situations a mare had lost her little one and realized her baby was dead.

Early one morning I arrived at the farm, where I was boarding, to find a mare foaling. She was having a difficult time. I called the veterinarian, but had to help some on my own. The colt was weak and not breathing well. We performed first aid techniques, and, in the meantime, I moved the mare to an adjoining stall. When it was obvious we could do no more for the little fellow, I went in to the mare. She was leaning against the stall wall and tears were streaming down her cheeks.

In another case a young filly had been allowed to breed far too young. Her foal was born deformed with no hope of leading a normal life. The little one could not control her hindquarters. It was obvious she would never be able to stand or walk. There were also respiratory problems. The decision was finally made to put the little fellow to sleep. The young filly threw herself against the wall and screamed so violently that she had to be tied and tranquilized to keep her from hurting herself.

A friend told me of her gelding that was in the field with an older mare that was much taller than he was. The Morgan gelding was a jumper and often went over the fence to another pasture. These two horses had been together for over two years and were close companions.

He jumped over one morning and apparently the mare tried to follow. There was a tree with low hanging branches along the fence. The gelding went under the branches, but the taller mare hit a branch and broke her neck. My friend found her gelding standing over the body of his friend and shedding tears.

Others have told me of similar experiences, therefore, it is reasonable to assume that some horses do feel love and know what has happened.

If the eyelid of the horse is torn or damaged, don't try to pull at it. Call the veterinarian immediately to sew it and treat the wound. If he has fallen or run into something sharp injuring the eyeball, he will be frantic with pain. Don't make it worse by yelling, chasing or hitting him. Be calm; get him calm and into a clean stall away from drafts or excitement. Don't try to wrestle with him to get a halter on. It does not necessarily mean the horse will lose his vision. If the eye is injured to the point that it is bleeding, remember he is not only in pain but is frightened and bewildered because he does not understand what is happening to him. Don't try to be your own veterinarian and cause more damage. Stand to his side and gently stroke his neck talking quietly.

Horses can have <u>CATARACTS</u> of the eye which is like a membrane that does not allow light to pass through and affects the lens. As of the writing of this book, there is no success in treating cataracts in a horse's eye. It does not mean he will lose his vision. Each case is different according to the breed, size of the animal and most importantly, his age.

<u>CONJUNCTIVITIS</u> Is usually a germ infection or can be caused by dirt and foreign matter irritating the eye causing it to water constantly. If this is not corrected, the discharge becomes thick and sticky. As a first aid, the eye can be washed with a solution made from a teaspoon of table salt to a pint of slightly warm water. Stir it thoroughly and apply it carefully so as not to cause further damage. The eye is so delicate. Always consult a veterinarian.

<u>MOON BLINDNESS</u> is an inflammation of the eye that occurs at regular intervals. Not enough is known about this disease, but we do know that it is not contagious. It does seem to be hereditary. The upper eyelids will droop and water freely. Light bothers the animal. Eventually the eyes become a bluish white and the animal slowly loses its eyesight. There is no sure cure. Keep the animal out of bright sunlight. Use a recommended eye lotion daily and keep the eye free of dust and irritants.

Sometimes eye lashes will turn inwards on the eye causing an inflammation. A veterinarian will trim the eyelashes short and suggest an eye lotion. In rare cases, a foal might be born with eyelids turned in. The veterinarian will perform a minor surgery to correct this.

Whatever the problem, remember the eye is tender and easily hurt, just as yours is. Check the eyes daily. Keep the face clean with cool water and a clean, white cloth.

TEETH

All horses, regardless of sex, are termed aged after nine years of age. Teeth must be kept healthy or the animal cannot eat properly or may suffer from digestive problems. The teeth continue growing and wear sharp. The tongue can be cut or cause difficulty in eating. Your veterinarian will float (file down) the teeth. Laugh if you will, but I do brush my horse's teeth with a regular brush like the one I use. They can get cavities and abscess.

Cherokee getting his teeth brushed. He likes it.

When a foal is born, it may have two tiny teeth or they may not appear for the first week. It is possible to sometimes find three cheek teeth. Observe a young horse. When they approach an older horse, they will open the mouth and rapidly click their teeth. This is their way of saying, "See, I'm just a baby. Please don't hurt me." It is rare that an older horse will hurt a baby. Sometimes a nursing dam, or one with foal fever, will be irritable or sometimes a jealous stallion will be temperamental with babies. In rare cases a mare might refuse to accept her baby and will hurt it if it comes to nurse. The little fellow must be raised on a bottle and cared for by a human, unless another mare with milk will accept it. I've known of people who let a goat step up on a raised surface and the baby would nurse from the goat.

Young horses usually have twenty-four temporary teeth. Twelve of these are incisors and twelve are molars. The front ones are lost as they mature just as human children lose their teeth. A mature mare will normally have thirty-six teeth while the mature male will have forty.

Permit me to share a funny experience. When I bought my first horse I did not know that they lost teeth. I guess I just assumed the teeth grew in and stayed. One morning I went out early to feed and found him with blood on his mouth and a loose tooth. I frantically called my veterinarian stating that some horse in the pasture had apparently fought my horse and kicked him in the mouth. That compassionate man rushed out even though he had started to eat his breakfast. When he saw the problem he howled with laughter and never let me forget it. He gave me the tooth and told me to wash the gums with warm salt water. He also said if the horse appeared to be having pain growing teeth, to rub the gums with paregoric on my finger. My silly, spoiled horse would see me coming with the bottle in my hand and would come to meet me with his mouth open wanting his gums massaged.

The tooth is made up of the root which is set in the bone in a socket called the alveolus and the outer portion which we can see. The end of the tooth is called the crown. The neck is the part near the gums. The covering is called enamel. Under the enamel is the dentine and in the center is the pulp cavity.

The temporary teeth, or milk teeth, of the young are called the deciduous and the permanent teeth are called the persistent. The incisor teeth are the twelve in front. The canine or tushes are farther back. These are found in the male although in some rare cases the canines have been found in a mare. The twenty-four molars are at the back and are often called the cheek teeth. These are what farmers call the grass-grinders.

When a horse begins to get his permanent teeth, you can see a small hollow, called a cup, on his incisors. As the teeth mature and slowly wear down, the cups vanish. At about seven years of age, the center front cups start wearing away and by the age of about twelve, the cups are gone.

At about nine or ten years, a groove appears on the incisors as a notch on the outer edge. This groove is called galvayne's groove. The galvayne's groove gradually travels down until about twenty years of age. The groove then starts disappearing from the top slowly working to the bottom where it disappears entirely at about thirty years of age.

Thus, if you check the teeth, you can be reasonably sure how old the horse is. A veterinarian can tell you for sure.

The first premolar is sometimes called the wolf tooth. As the horse ages, the incisors will slant outward and look more narrow. The gums begin to shrink making the teeth appear to be longer. The health of the animal, the type of food he has customarily eaten and the type of grazing he has done, will determine how quickly the teeth wear and slant. Naturally the harder a horse has to live, the worse his teeth will become.

The foal has two central incisors and usually three cheek teeth. By age one month to one and a half month, the lateral incisors cut through. By age one (yearling) all incisors are through as well as four cheek teeth. A rising two (almost two years old) will be filling in with more molars. It is all right to start teaching him to hold a bit in his mouth now.

The animal may sometimes have an inflammation of the mouth caused by some foreign object either cutting or causing an irritation around the teeth, gums, tongue or inside the cheek. It could be a sharp thorn or a hard piece of hay. Putting a bit in the mouth too soon can cause problems with the mouth and teeth.

If the gums, lips, tongue or cheek are swollen and redder than usual, or if there is an extra amount of saliva and trouble in eating or drinking, check to see what is causing the trouble. It may be something you can remove or treat. Give the horse fresh, cold water. Feed soft feeds. If the symptoms do not disappear, call the veterinarian. Sometimes an ulcer will form at the root of a decayed tooth. If the horse develops bad breath, trouble chewing or it stays swollen, call the veterinarian immediately. If allowed to go untreated, the horse will not eat or drink and cannot rest. The tooth will probably have to be removed. If not treated, you could lose a valuable animal.

Again, put yourself in the animal's place. How would you like to be ignored with a cavity, abscess or puncture of some kind in your mouth?

CRIBBING

Cribbing is biting on stall sides, fences, or anything available. It is a very bad habit usually caused by boredom. This can lead to serious digestive disorders due to the fact that the animal is sucking in a lot of air and filling the stomach in an unnatural manner. Smear creosote on the areas where he is biting or some bitter medicine that will discourage the habit. If this does not work, a cribbing strap will need to be buckled around the throat.

I put big beach balls for them to kick and chase, hang empty cans from trees for them to butt and play with or a barrel to roll in the paddock or pasture.

WIND SUCKING

Wind sucking is similar to cribbing except the animal does not bite. He hooks his front upper teeth over the edge of a fence, or an object, pulls back and drags in a big gulp of air. It sounds awful and looks worse. He can damage his teeth, but the biggest damage will be to his stomach and intestines. If a lot of wind is dragged in, it can cause colic. The cribbing strap works most of the time.

In the event that you have a valuable show animal that is injured or has to be stalled, or a stallion that is kept in a small enclosure, there are things you can do to relieve the boredom. Hang clean empty plastic jugs from a heavy string for him to bump with his nose and play with it. Be careful that it is an object that will not break, splinter, or tempt him to make a snack of it. Your animal is helpless and depending upon you to be considerate of him.

We kept a female goat with our little Arabian stallion or any injured horse that had to be stalled. Gud Flicka (Swiss for good little girl) was a delight to people and animals. You can rotate horses to stay in nearby stalls to relieve boredom. I also keep a small battery-powered radio out of the way of curious animals, but playing music. We found that all music stations were obviously appreciated. Cherokee sways to the music. This is not only entertainment, but it gets them accustomed to hearing noises. When they are taken out in public, they're less likely to be shy and act silly.

FEEDING

The natural means for a horse to eat is to forage or graze. We humans took this natural method away by building and cultivating on the grazing and forest lands. This is sad in many ways. We not only took away natural homes and food of the animals, but have also damaged and destroyed our own resources for the future. Plants and trees give off oxygen that we need, and absorb carbon dioxide and many elements that are harmful to us.

Due to the increase in our population, and to the needed space for homes and businesses, we have taken a tremendous amount of land. Therefore, it is our duty and responsibility to provide space for our animals to live and provide adequate, nutritional food for them.

Horses absolutely need the bulk and roughage for efficient digestion. This must be provided in addition to grain and vitamins. If there is no available pasture, or if it is during the time of year when pasture is unavailable, we must feed a good, quality hay that has been cut and stored by a reputable dealer or a trustworthy person. Just giving the animal something to fill the stomach is not providing adequate hay. If you do not know how to check the hay, have someone who is knowledge check it for nutritional value and taste. Twice this fall I visited stables that assumed good quality hay had been purchased when, in fact, they had paid for something of no value. The stable owners had not only lost a good deal of money, but their horses, and their boarders, had no hay for a few days. A better grade was found two days later.

In one case a woman though she had gotten a real bargain by buying a ton of hay for ninety-five cents a bale. When I looked at it, I was sick at heart. She had bought a load of barley straw with a few leaves. This week a friend asked me to come to the stable where she, and other boarders, had complained about mold, dust and a terrible odor about the hay. I found thick pieces of stem, a few pieces of damp and coarse grass and lots of weeds and trash. The hay was not only moldy, dusty and dangerous for the animals to eat, but it had absolutely no nutritional value. The grain was being stored in a hot area with little air and was of poor quality; very cheap. Their horses were getting their stomachs filled, but were slowly starving to death. The stable owner, apparently, had not cared. I left them with the suggestion to find another stable they could trust, ask for their money back and threaten to sue. At any rate report it to an interested newspaper reporter and make the facts known to the public. This might save another innocent owner, maybe even a young person with their first horse.

Good hay includes legume, grasses and often a mixture of the two. Legume hays are higher in calcium, protein and carotene. (Carotene is the precursor of Vitamin A.) This tastes better to the animal and makes excellent feeding for horses whether young, working or in a breeding program. Although grasses are easier to grow and supply quantity, check for quality. If fields where good grasses are grown are turned (plowed), fertilized and seeded on a regular basis, one can get a good crop of quality hay. The grass must not be allowed to mature too long before being cut if quality is desired.

Orchard grass can be a mixture of clover, timothy, oats, barley, wheat, rye and other types which grow in that particular area. I don't mean all of these must be grown at the same time or fed at the same time.

Timothy is lower in protein, and, therefore, is more suitable for mature horses rather than young horses or breeding animals. Be careful though, for too much timothy can cause overheating and the animal will have more energy than the means of getting rid of it.

A good legume is alfalfa. If it is properly cured, it is high in calcium, carotene and protein. This is given to brood mares, young horses in training as well as show horses that are worked on a regular basis. The high protein count makes it dangerous for the kidneys of a horse that does not work it off.

Lespedeza must be cut early to make excellent hay. It is good bulk, but only contains half as much calcium as alfalfa. If it is allowed to mature, it had little nutritional value and the stems become wiry and low in digestibility.

Properly cured red clover is a good item for mixed hay. Clovers are lower in protein and have more leaves and stems. The horses love the taste of it but may not be getting adequate nutritional value with too much clover. Also, older horses, or those that are not worked much, may slobber a lot with clover. They could develop loose bowels and be uncomfortable as well as sick.

In Virginia, my pleasure horses got a mixture of timothy, clover and grasses. Here in Florida, I have had to feed some African Star and Bermuda. In my own pasture I planted Bahia, oats, rye and white clover. The clover did not do well, the rye only grows in cooler months, but the Bahia and oats have come up well.

When I first moved to Florida, I went to the Agricultural Office and asked for advice on what to plant and feed. My land was twenty acres, eighteen of them pure dirt. I hired a man to plow under fifty tons of chicken manure and items suggested by the Agriculture Department. We had ninety days of drought immediately following, so I had to start from scratch again. Eventually I did get a beautiful grazing ground with nice, big oak trees. I fenced off half an acre and plowed that under using the manure and straw left from the stalls. I planted vegetables and watermelons. I got more vegetables than we could keep up with and we were still using watermelon that following Thanksgiving when we had the whole family in for dinner. Those late watermelons came from the seeds we had thrown out after eating earlier melons.

We hired a man to build a stable using the drawings I had made. Our front lawn was a whole acre and the rest I planted in flowers and roses. We both loved this "ranch" of ours, but my husband only got to enjoy it for six years until he died much too young and too early.

The statement, "eats like a horse" is misused. They prefer to eat small amounts several times a day. Keep plenty of fresh water available at all time. We bought a large galvanized tub, big enough for a bath tub, and sat it under a faucet. It made it easier to keep water fresh for them. I was amazed one morning to find that it was cold enough (in Florida?!) to freeze the top of the water. Cherokee called it to my attention by putting one front hoof on the ice and trying to punch through it.

If you don't have water except in the stall buckets, give water before feeding. Hay should be given before grain so that the bulk of the hay will not force the grain through the digestive system before nutritional value is gained from it.

NEVER work an animal after eating as the digestive system needs the muscles to make sure the food is being used properly all over the body for growth, muscles, bones, blood circulation and energy. Wait at least an hour.

Make sure your horses are wormed about every three months depending upon the type of ground, feed and working conditions. Consult the veterinarian for this. The teeth should be checked and floated as often as necessary. Teeth in need of care can cause a well-fed horse to starve because he cannot utilize his food properly.

Oats and other cereal grain are high in energy food. They cause inner heat and energy. If the horse is not exercised and worked regularly, he will be flighty and an overactive animal that is a problem in any situation because he has too much energy and needs to burn it off --- just like young children.

A regular feeding program is most important. The digestive juices flow at the proper times and the animal is relaxed and ready to allow his body to use his food properly if fed on schedule. If he worries and gets hungry and wonders when he is going to get fed, it upsets his digestive system.

Some horses are "easy keepers" which means they do not need as much food at one time as another horse might. Just as some people stay healthy and keep their weight even on small, but well-balanced meals. Some animals, and people, can eat a lot and not gain weight while others eat less and gain rapidly. Know what is best for your animal. Feed according to the type of work being done, the breed, age and health levels.

Along with water, salt must be available at all times. Salt is important to the entire body. Mineral salt licks are good. A small salt block can be in the stall or a large one out in the pasture. If salt is given just when the person thinks of it, the horse might gulp too much water and suffer. This would cause a shock to the body's system and might even cause colic. A horse that is sick or hot after being worked, should be given small amounts of water often. Fresh running water is, of course, the best.

While visiting some ranches in the western states, I was told that since hay is hard to grow, the ranchers buy cubes of compressed hay from Mexico. There is no waste and the horses eat at a rate that is good for their digestion. Also, the cubes are easier to store and handier to feed. Water was brought in by a long system of pipes.

No one food by itself is a totally good food any more than it would be if a person ate one food all day, every day.

Oats can be rolled, flaked or crimped as well as whole. The whole oats are the best because they are not as full of dust and offer more bulk. However, few horses will chew whole oats well. Oats are high in protein but tend to produce a lot of heat and energy just as corn does.

Molasses are often added to mixed grain to make it taste better and make it easier to handle. Molasses has about eighty percent as much nutritional value as most of the grains. It should not be included in the feed in hot weather because the horses do not need the extra heat or energy.

Soybean meal is high in T D N (Total Digestible Nutrients) and is very good to mix with other feed, especially bran. Bran is the coarse outer covering of wheat. It offers good bulk and acts as a laxative. Do not give it to growing young horses often as it will be too harsh for their system.

Barley packs down and can cause colic if not digested properly. It is a good grain but should be mixed with other gains, especially more palatable ones.

Be very careful about giving your horse a cob with corn on it. Most of them will eat the corn off the cob, but once in a while an animal will try to eat the cob and get it stuck in the throat. As a horse cannot vomit, or bring anything up, he could choke to death. Additionally, a corn cob is hard to digest.

In the spring I add a tablespoon of linseed meal to each feeding for about a month. This helps the animal shed the old winter coat and gives luster to the new one. Never feed a large amount of linseed meal, cottonseed or peanut oil, all of which can cause digestive problems. They are good for nursing mares and mares in foal. Check with your veterinarian before giving anything to a horse.

Old horses, horses with teeth problems, or horses that have been sick or injured are often given hot food. Cooked grains are more digestible than otherwise, but cooking does take away some of the nutritional value. Bran mash is often given to sick or old animals. It is sometimes given to horses after a hard day of hunting or working in the field. Once a week a bran mash is good for almost every horse. Again, consult your veterinarian. Remember, it works on the bowels so don't expect your horse to go out the next day and do a lot of work after a bran mash.

Cooked barley is an excellent means of putting weight on a thin or sick horse. It is also good for the coat of show horses. Do not feed more than twice a week and use only whole barley cooked until the husk cracks.

Calf Manna can be used to feed a growing horse, a mare in foal, or a nursing mare. Beet pulp is low in protein but is a good fiber material. It is often added to feed of horses that are allergic to feeds and is also good for old horses. Only use beet pulp as a supplement and not as a total feed. It does require a lot of water with it.

Check with your veterinarian as to vitamins that are necessary for your particular horse. Some will need them year round, while others only during special periods of time.

I feed Vi-Pro-Min with mixed feed because I have found that it suits my purpose for nutrition and for an excellent aid in building a good coat. It brings out the color in a horse, especially the Palomino.

Clovite is a popular vitamin but it is actually a hormonal supplement. It helps regulate the fertility cycle. Whatever you use, keep it in metal containers with tightly closed lids. If feed is left open, rodents will feel free to help themselves, leaving droppings and germs in the food. All kinds of parasites, molds or rust can be found in grains. If you find it

-- throw it away where it can't be eaten. IT CAN KILL. New food is cheaper then replacing a much loved animal.

Whatever you decide to feed (after you and your veterinarian have consulted on it) and whatever schedule you work out that is best for the animal and you -- stick to it. Don't be tempted to skip a feeding because you are tired, discouraged or even sick. Know someone close by you can call and ask to feed for you if you positively can't. Regardless of how you feel, the animal still gets hungry and needs the energy from the food. It is much kinder and loving to the animal to care for it daily on a regular basis. If you can't, please love it enough to allow someone to take of it who can feed, groom, exercise and care for it medically, rather than to satisfy a selfish human desire to have an animal. This is true of all pets.

BEDDING AND BARN MANAGEMENT

Again, I shall touch upon the most important items and cannot include all of the minute, pertinent details that could otherwise be in this chapter. The stall must be absolutely dry, clean with good ventilation and without being drafty. If there are animals in adjoining stalls, and there is a partition with an open top, place wire or something up there so that animals can see each other but cannot bite or cause injury to one another.

Like most people, animals are gregarious and need friends. Sometimes they form a bond that makes it next to impossible to separate them.

Urine and manure contain ammonia. Dirty stalls will have plenty of this. Do not leave it in a stall for more than as few hours as you can manage. It can cause serious hoof problems. Should an animal try to lie down in urine and manure bedding, he can get serious skin burns, eye irritation and respiratory diseases.

A stall should be cleaned all the way down to the main surface at least twice a week. This may have to be done more often if the animal is stalled all the time due to an injury or sickness, or if he is a valuable animal that the owner doesn't want to risk running out in the open. Otherwise the stall should be picked up daily with manure piles and wet areas completely cleaned out. All rocks or uneven surfaces should be removed. If there are too many deep, large rocks or uneven surfaces, then extra dirt and clay should be brought in and tamped down to cover this hard material.

When the stall is cleaned all the way down to the main surface, then a coating of powdered lime, especially for this purpose, should be spread evenly over the surface to help kill germs and sweeten the stall. I also wash down the walls with hot water and Lysol, then rinse with warm water. Naturally the horse is not in the stall during this time. The stall should then be allowed to "sit" for several hours with good ventilation so it can air out and dry thoroughly.

Straw is the most widely used bedding. This can be bad though because it holds the urine and other dirty substances. It also allows the bad to leak through to the bottom where it becomes a dangerous area for growth of infections. Additionally the worst part is, the animal might be tempted to eat the straw and will then have nothing to protect him from the air along the floor or rough surfaces.

Wood shavings and sawdust will soak up a lot of the moisture and can be cleaned easier with a daily cleaning. The sawdust is also warmer for the animal. Beware of urine soaked sawdust packing in the hoof and causing thrush or similar diseases. The sawdust should be free of a lot of dust and should smell clean. Peat is the very best bedding, but it is next to impossible to obtain here in the United States.

Sand is used in some areas for bedding but this holds too much moisture and unsanitary materials. Also, it is hard on the horse's skin and terrible to groom out of the coat. If a bored animal, or one that is not being fed properly, is tempted to eat the sand, he can have serious stomach and bowel problems and the threat of colic is always present.

Shredded paper and crushed peanut shells are used in some areas. Regardless of the bedding, clean it every day. The health of your animal depends upon you. NEVER USE OLD, MOLDY HAY OR DRY DUSTY BEDDING.

The dirty and used material should be taken well away from the stalls so that the animals are not walking in it or lying down in it. Keep it away from grazing areas where it is possible to spread worms and many diseases. A special machine for grinding and spreading manure and dirty materials as fertilizer can be used in areas to help the grass grow. If you can rotate grazing areas, keep the animals away while you plow this manure under and allow good grass to grow.

To clean properly daily, rake the clean material to one side. Take out the dirty material and let the floor air out. Then rake the clean material over this and place a new and clean top layer.

Bedding should be about four inches deep or at least deep enough to make a comfortable sleeping area. It is wise to place the animal out in pasture or in a paddock while the stall is being cleaned. Groom the horse well and clean his hooves before placing him in a clean stall again.

Establish a good routine for your barn work and training sessions and you'll find that time is saved without pressure. I could not afford to hire full-time workers, so I was thankful for teen volunteers who worked in exchange for free lessons and an occasional trail ride. I sometimes allow a few of them to show a horse.

While in Virginia, I taught school and my husband worked several miles away in Washington, D.C. We both worked a long day including traveling time. We would get up about 4 AM and go to the horses. According to the weather, we would either feed each horse in its own stall or tie it to a fence in front of a feed bucket. While they were eating we would wash water tubs and fill them with clean water, stalls were cleaned and hay was placed either in racks or out in the pasture. We would check each horse for cuts, bruises or anything that needed attention. We then washed the feeding tubs or buckets, and finally made our way back home for showers, breakfast and off to work. Sixteen-hour days of work were usual with us.

I know we did not give the hay first, but in our case we did not have the time to wait for them to eat the hay and then give grain. Give a couple more flakes of hay when feeding in the pasture than the number of horses. Then the bullies cannot chase a timid one entirely from hay.

Each weekend we stripped the stalls clean to the floor and cleaned them properly.

Each evening after work, we fed and cleaned all over again. As time permitted we rode and exercised or trained, cleaned and groomed properly, checked tack in need of repair and any other work required.

I would take a wide bamboo rake and rake the aisles and walking area to give the stable a neat appearance. One should take as much pride in the appearance of the animals and stables as one's personal appearance.

NEVER allow running or loud, unnecessary noises around the stalls. It is unsafe and undesirable. NEVER allow smoking or drinking because of the danger involved. Fires are something that can be avoided unless it's lightning. Drinking causes a person to not show the best common sense when working with animals.

Areas where you ride or exercise regularly should be checked often. Extra time is better than an infection or injuries.

EMOTIONS

Even though you may love animals and have your heart set on owning a horse, fear or insecurity may be a strong emotion to overcome. Inexperience and uncertainty can cause panic in many people. Don't be ashamed to admit your fear or uncertainty. The animal will sense it and you'll have more trouble than you counted on having.

I have observed people approach a horse looking determined, but feeling jumpy inside. The animal doesn't know the person is afraid of him. His reaction will be: "Fear! Something to be afraid of! Where?" The horse jumps or moves suddenly and the person, already jittery, will jump and sometimes foolishly scream. They stand there jumping at each other, accomplishing nothing.

An inexperienced or uncertain person should be paired with a wise old horse that can teach the person until he or she is ready for a more challenging animal.

I was so proud of one of the mothers. She brought her two-year-old daughter to me to learn to ride. The mother admitted that she was even afraid to be in the area. Fortunately I had a gentle pony with a lot of experience. I had the mother just walk around him and pet him first with me beside her. She then learned to use a brush on the pony. Before a month had passed she was leading the pony alone and doing a great job. Best of all she loved it. She admitted she never wanted to ride but asked if she could groom more horses and help. That little girl did so well that she entered shows and earned several blue ribbons. She had even started one-foot high jumping when she had to leave me. She was a very mature little girl. Several years went by and, much to my surprise, I received an invitation to her wedding. Surely not. It was true, and I have many lovely memories of that precious little girl.

I also had the two-year-old little boy, the son of a prominent doctor in town. He too did well, but not as well as the little girl.

Allow me to share a humiliating experience. There was no excuse for me because I knew better. I purchased a rising three-year-old Palomino gelding (nearing three) from Arthur Godfrey. We named him Meloso D'Oro, meaning like honey of the gold. He was anything but. I did not know that for the first two years of his life he had been allowed to roam in the field without real training. He was not accustomed to discipline and training. I am firm but not cruel. Firm does not mean punishment. It means asking him to learn a lesson and not giving in until he has learned it well. Meloso resented the consistent work.

I started lunging him and getting him acquainted with my voice. He bitterly resented these training sessions and proceeded to charge me with teeth, feet and body slams. I foolishly had nothing with which to protect myself except the end of the lunge line. I could never have done it intentionally, but I jumped backward over a five-foot fence while he crashed screaming into the fence and tearing at it. I had handled many young horses, and older ones who needed retraining. Nothing like this.

I knew better than to back down like that, but it was a shock. This became a game for Meloso. He was smart enough to try to bully me even when I was feeding him.

Two days after that incident, I was crossing Meloso's private paddock with a gallon bucket carrying grain to him. He charged and backed me against the barn wall. He paid no attention to my commands to back and stand ho. As he reared over me trying to put me down with his front feet, I slung that bucket up as hard as I could into his chest and made myself speak softly and calmly. He just got madder and sank his teeth into my arm. I was finally able to keep him at bay until I could again get over that fence. I had bruises all over me. Believe me as I truthfully say, I never was afraid of him, but he's the only horse with whom I've never fallen in love.

The next day I called the veterinarian. After checking Meloso he found that he had been badly gelded, meaning someone had botched the job. He had part of his testicles removed, but all of the glands were not cleaned out so that he still had the desire to mate and was frustrated because he couldn't. He was a ridgling or proud cut.

Even when Meloso was cross-tied and being groomed, he still fought with teeth, feet and tried body slams. It usually took three people to groom him, especially to clean his feet. He did not fight the saddle being placed on his back, but he did fight being mounted. Once I was on his back he was smooth and quick to learn. However, I prayed constantly that nothing would happen to get me off of him as I knew what the results would be.

He discovered he could not unseat me by bucking and running, so he began rearing straight up. I was afraid he would fall over with me and hurt himself, but I guess he was too smart for that. I asked a wise old black trainer of Thoroughbreds what I should do. He said, "Missy, let that sucker come up, then you pick a soft spot to land, jump off and pull him over. When he lands, sit on his head and cuss him out big and loud." As he reared one day, I did jump off and pulled him over, but I didn't have to sit on his head or say anything. He had bitten his own tongue and it scared him so badly he never reared again.

The next time I visited Mr. Godfrey, I told him of the problems. He laughed that laugh that I'm sure all of you remember. He said, "Huh, Huh. If anyone can handle him you can Sioux." Thanks a lot.

Arthritis began to trouble me so I could not work the horses as I would have liked or needed to do. A young county policeman was willing to come out and ride as I told him. He did very well. Also, a girlfriend and her husband came to the stable often. We found that Meloso responded to her husband so well that I finally sold him to them. Meloso made an excellent trail horse for him and was a winner and in the top horses in the Old Dominion Endurance Rides.

Thus, I learned the hard way that some horses do prefer one gender to another. While my Cherokee plainly liked women better, he was never mean with anyone.

Harsh punishment would have only built a stronger resentment in this horse. He required firm, consistent training and a longer period of time than I have ever used in training. This is why we need to experiment with each

82

animal to determine the best training method for that particular animal.

Discipline <u>must be given</u> at the exact moment of disobedience. Otherwise, like a small child, he will assume you're just being cruel and unfair. Praise should be given at the exact moment of good behavior or learning to reinforce the need to please and to learn.

If you discipline or punish an animal (or a child) just because you're angry, frustrated, impatient or immature, they will not trust you or any other human. They might develop a jumping shyness or throwing the head around.

One horse I own is so sensitive that a harsh voice will make him tremble and almost crawl asking for forgiveness even though he has done nothing wrong. He is eager to please and will move with springy steps and sparkling eyes if he is praised. Horses learn a lot from our own behavior. So control yourself first.

CATCHING, TYING, LEADING

Few horses come to you willingly if they are in an open area, especially if they are with other horses that have no reason to come to you. This is one time it would be all right to bribe your horse until he is trained to come to you. A carrot, apple, grain -- or in Cherokee's case, rosebuds, will encourage the animal. Just be careful that you don't have several animals bearing down on you at once. I am not in favor of using sugar. This is not only very poor nutritionally, but it often causes horses to start nipping at anyone around in hopes of getting sugar from them.

The best method is patience and time. Several times a day walk up to the animal with a choice bit of snack in your hand. Do not try to catch him. Give a low whistle or a call that you will use to call him. Pet his cheek and over his body. After a while stop a short distance from him, give the signal and hold the tid bit. Allow him to walk to you. Again pet and praise him.

Gradually increase the distance but not so far away that he'll feel it isn't worthwhile coming to you. This may take several tries and several days.

Finally try standing a greater distance and give your call. He'll learn that to come to you means getting something good to snack, in addition to being petted and groomed. Keep one hand on his shoulder while you hold the halter in the other hand. Gently lift the halter to go on him and help it on with the hand on his shoulder. Keep yourself near his shoulder so that he will not hurt you if he shows irritation by striking out with a hoof.

Massage his ears gently and take a few steps, holding the lead line with the hand that is away from the horse. Walk a few steps, speaking softly and praising him. If he is ever hurt, such as a pinched ear or a mouth hit with the metal bit, he will be wary about cooperating.

All this is done with a very young horse or with one that is new to you. Keep standing on his left side near his shoulder. If you need to turn him, turn <u>away</u> from you so that he won't climb up on your back if you turn him toward you.

At first do not work him every time you catch him. Lead him, speak softly, do a good grooming job and release him. He won't learn to dread seeing you coming. After a few days of this, teach him to be led from either the left or right side.

A skittish horse, or one who is untrained, may have to be tied as I do when training a young horse. First tie a rope to a stout fence or a tree. Tie the other end to an old tire. Tie the lead line to the other side of the tire. If he pulls back or fights, there is some give without him hurting himself. Also, a slip knot should be used whenever or wherever a horse is tied so that he can be released quickly in an emergency. (I'll show you later how to do this.)

Do not stand in front of a horse facing him and expect him to walk with you. As long as you are looking at him, he won't move. Turn your back to him, keep the lead line securely on your hand and walk. He'll follow.

Remember, horses are playful by nature. They play and push each other. When a horse is young, it may seem cute for him to run up and butt you with his head. As he grows and gets stronger, it isn't so funny. It is a dangerous habit. They feel they are dominating you.

Cherokee thought it was funny to sneak up behind my husband and "steal" his baseball cap off his head. He would dance around just out of reach. If Mike was hammering something and happened to lay the hammer down where Cherokee could see it, he would pick it up in his teeth and walk away. He knew he was playing with us. We played tag with him but did not allow him to run into us or push us.

When holding, or leading, a horse DO NOT wrap the line around your hand or tie it around your waist, as I've seen a few do. The most gentle, well-trained horse can spook at a strange happening or an unexpected noise and jerk back ready to run. You can be hurt badly.

When I only had the first two horses and was boarding in a stable, I was working in the indoor ring one morning. A high-ranking army officer came in leading a big Thoroughbred. He proceeded to lunge the horse around him at one end. He allowed too much line on the ground and the horse to come too close. I thought I was helping and said, "Sir, you might get caught in that line. You'd better shorten it or allow the horse to go out farther." He glared at me and continued. I went on with my business and it wasn't long until I heard a yell. That line had wrapped around one of his legs and he went down. His falling and yelling frightened the horse and he started pulling and running around the ring. I had a time trying to stop him. The man had a badly broken leg and pulled back muscles. Never be too arrogant to at least listen when someone is trying to help you.

When a horse has a habit of pulling or trying to break away, I have brought the line behind me and under my hips because then I have more leverage. But I never wrap the line around me.

If a horse has become a bully with humans, carry a rolled up newspaper. Snapping it in the air or popping him on the shoulder will usually work. If this is done while saying a firm, "NO," it will teach him that what he is doing is unacceptable.

People who whip horses are not only showing their own ignorance, but are doing one of two things: 1) the animal will only back down at the moment and wait to attack a human; or 2) his spirit will be broken and he'll be just a pokey, unhappy animal. Remember, punishment is not beating. It is firm discipline and must be given at the time of disobedience.

If a horse tries to nibble on you, don't smack at his head. He'll develop the bad habit of throwing his head. Push him away gently but firmly with a strong "NO." I don't advise everyone to do the following because it could be dangerous. If a horse has developed a tendency to bite, hold a <u>clean</u> new sharp nail in your hand so that only a small point is showing between the fingers. Don't throw your hand out at him, but when he sticks his neck out to bite, hold the hand steady and allow him to stick himself. He'll think he's the one who hurt himself and he won't try that again.

If a horse strikes out with a front hoof, keep a clean round stick in your hand. Don't hit at him, but hold the stick steady in your hand. When he strikes out, he'll think he has hurt himself.

When an animal tries to outrun me, I don't try to pull him back because weight is pulling against me. I run beside him and get near his head and then pull him around or try to lunge him. Don't yell, it will only excite him more. Speak softly and firmly.

No horse should be tied in such a way that he can't be released immediately. Practice tying slip knots that can be released if you pull the end, but if the horse pulls, he'll just tighten the knot.

Stand facing the rope and place it around whatever you're using as a tying station. Pass a long section of the end of the rope up past the attached end. Make a loop. Hold the end of the rope in your right hand... Place the left hand through the loop and take a section of the loose end in your left hand. Make a small loop in this section and bring it through the larger loop. Pull down on the attached end of the rope to tighten it and leave the end loose.

For a quick release, pull the loose end.

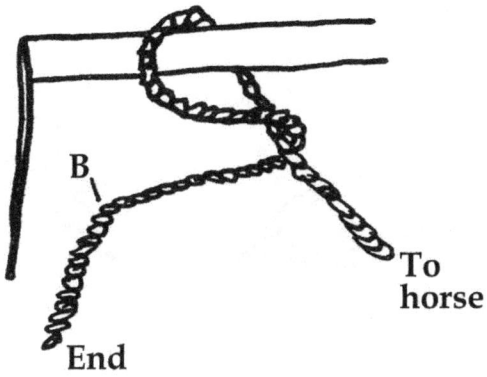

B

To
horse

End

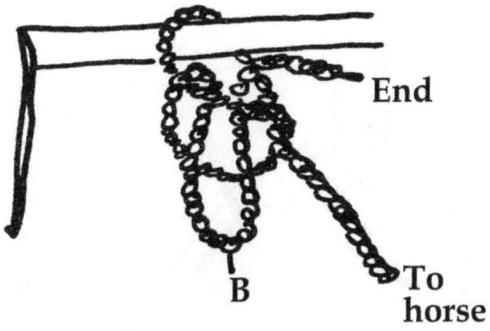

End

B

To
horse

There is one safe method I use for tying a skittish horse that has never been taught to tie quietly. First place the animal on grass, sand or a soft area where he won't hurt himself if he fights and falls over.

You will need at least a thirty-foot long cotton rope. Tie the rope around the horse's barrel, down between his front legs, up around his neck, under his chin, through the end of the halter ring and finally tie it to a stout object. Then if he pulls or "lays back" he will only pull on himself.

After he learns to stand tied without fighting, praise him and make him feel good that he has done something right. Slowly walk around him holding a saddle blanket. Let him smell it and look at it first. Lay it on his back and drag it off. Pull it across his neck, under his belly and all over him. He will learn that he can trust you and it isn't going to hurt him.

I have placed aluminum foil on fences, on gates and hanging from the door going into the stable. He will learn to accept strange things without being frightened. I also have a radio playing music so that he can get accustomed to noise. This is good especially if you expect to ride him in parades or in a show. Tie aluminum plates swinging on low branches so that he won't be afraid of objects moving around him.

Slow, patient training keeps him calm and easier to handle. If you want to show in a trail class, or go on trail rides, you want to be prepared for rain. Hold a plastic raincoat in front of him so that he can see and smell it. Put it on and off so that he'll learn the noise won't hurt him. Later, while riding, put the raincoat on and off slowly so that he doesn't get frightened.

New bridles, saddles, grooming equipment, or anything used on him, should be held for him to see and smell first. Like a small child, the horse will be eager to please and willingly work with you if you don't rush him or scare him. If you tease him, it will only build a lack of trust in you and all humans.

I can't say enough that training should take time, patience and love.

GROOMING

An excellent way to get an animal accustomed to being handled is by grooming. This is pleasure for the animal and good for the person. For the unsure, insecure person, grooming builds confidence.

Grooming daily is just as important as a person bathing, brushing teeth and combing hair. Grooming makes an animal feel better and aids in the blood circulation. It helps the animal's coat look and feel healthy. Also, this is a good time to check your entire horse to make sure he is free of cuts, bruises and doesn't have a fever.

Cross-tying is the best means of grooming, however any method that is satisfactory to the animal and you is acceptable. Do not tie under a low ceiling or branches where he might get excited and rear causing an injury to himself. Freak accidents do happen.

Before you begin bathing or grooming, bring everything you will need where you are working to save you running back and forth. After finishing, clean and wipe down anything you used so the items stay usable and won't wear out quickly. Place everything back where it belongs so that it can be found for the next time.

For the weekly bath, I use a no tears shampoo for the face and head and Ivory liquid soap over the body. Under some circumstances, such as a skin rash, the veterinarian may recommend another type of soap. For the mane and tail I use the same cream rinse that I use on my hair, being careful to rinse thoroughly with clear water. A strong stream of warm water from a hose makes a good massage when used in a circular motion.

If coming to the animal from the rear or side, speak to him and let him known you're there. He could be taking a nap and you would startle him to kick or jump.

Use voice commands that you'll use when on his back. For instance if you want him to move to one side, gently push on the side where your foot and stirrup would normally be, and say, "Over." If he gets frightened or acts up, use the command you'll use to calm him, such as, "Easy, easy," or "Stand ho."

Always check and clean the feet whether you're preparing to ride or not. Do clean the feet after each ride. Each person develops their own process of grooming. I start by washing the face and gently rubbing the ears out and nostrils with a clean cloth. I then wash under the tail and the sheath of a male or the teats of a female. Then I brush the body thoroughly. Make sure you clear the elbow and joint areas.

Please do not work an animal into a sweat and then just turn him loose. Dirt and sweat is very uncomfortable. Walk him until he cools down. Then rub a soft cloth over the whole boy. Sometimes you may want to use water to rinse him off. Put yourself in the horse's place. How would like to be forced to run or work until you're sweating and dirty and then just set out to do the best you can.

The hard rubber, or plastic, currycomb is ideal for combing the mane and tail as it does not break the hair and pull as much as a mane comb does. The currycomb can be used along with the dandy brush to bring dirt and grime to the surface of the hair so that it can be brushed away with a body brush. Do not use hard bristles around soft areas such as the face, legs and back section of the belly.

Brushing deeply is important because the dirt can just be pushed deeper into the hair and cause skin infections unless you use strong circular motions with a lot of 'elbow grease'. A good, clean sponge is best for the soft areas. Keep old towels to be used for polishing cloths.

The sweat scraper is for scraping off sweat and excess moisture after a bath. I use the scraper and shedding blade for a lot of my grooming, especially in the spring when he is shedding.

All brushes should be combed out and then washed with warm, soapy water and rinsed well. Lay them in the air to dry, bristles up. Keep all grooming equipment clean and put it back where it belongs when you've finished.

BRAIDING

There may be a time when you want to braid the mane and/or tail. The mane is simple to braid. Pull the hairs until the mane is not long and dragging and the ends are even. Wash the hair and rinse carefully. Using the mane comb, separate a small section, about one inch wide, and keep the rest out of the way by leaving the comb holding it back. Braid just as you would a child's hair. If you're showing remember, an even number of braid for a filly, or mare and an uneven number of braids for a male.

At the end of the braid I usually took a needle and thread and sewed it together and then turned it under and sewed it to the other side. Then I tied a very small bow around it. Do as you please. Rubber bands break the hair.

If the mane is too thick, ragged and uneven, you will need to comb the mane down smoothly. Take the longer hairs in your fingers and push the others up out of the way. Pull the longer hairs. There are no nerve endings, so you won't hurt the horse. He might object to the force of the pull, but he won't fight. <u>Do not cut with scissors</u> or the hair will grow in thicker and become unmanageable.

If you want a fancy lattice-work braid, you will need to get someone to show you in person for I cannot tell you in enough detail on paper.

Sometimes a person might braid the mane of a Western horse, at home just to get the hair to lie correctly. A lot of

Western horses have roached or cut mane all the way to the neck.

The bridle path of all horses should be trimmed smoothly. This is the hair at the top of the neck just behind the ears. Cut all the way down to the neck so that the top of the bridle fits smoothly and does not rub the hair on his neck. It looks much neater to trim about two or three inches.

If you're using electric equipment, don't surprise the horse with it. Turn it on and hold it in front of him so that he can see it and know it won't hurt him. Hold it in your hand and place the back of your hand on him so that he feels the vibration, but not the instrument. If he accepts this, then turn the hand over and start trimming. Don't rush him or you'll always have trouble. Use the currycomb then to brush out and proceed with the rest of the grooming, bathing or braiding.

The tail of the English horse can be put up in a variety of ways. If a horse is likely to kick, either Western or English horse, be a responsible owner and tie a big red bow on your horse's tail near the rump. This alerts people that they should not get behind that horse or crowd him.

A simple braid for an English horse's tail is like a child's. Comb out well and make sure the hair is clean. Divide into three strips and go to it. Start high on the tail. Bring the left strip over the middle and the right over the middle. Go all the way down to the bottom and either braid in a ribbon and then tie it or sew it. Remember, rubber bands are not good for the hair. This braid can just hang down or roll it under up to the rump and tie it off.

Fancy braiding will have to be taught in person. Always roll the tail up when shipping.

Let me warn you about using sharp instruments to get bot fly eggs off the horse. There is an instrument especially for that --- not a razor or the open edge of scissors. Hot water mixed with lots of vinegar will usually help get rid of these as well.

TACK AND CARE

Tack is the equipment you'll use on your horse such as the saddle and bridle. The type of tack you use will depend on several things. Are you going to ride English or Western or both? As I've said, I ride English, Western and side saddle. Therefore, I need different saddles, different bridles, different clothes, and well -- you get the idea. Will you be riding strictly for your own pleasure, for showing, for jumping ----? Each will require different tack. Yes, this can get expensive, but with proper care, it will last a long time.

Not all saddles fit just any horse. Be careful that yours is well fitted or the animal will be uncomfortable and might even be hurt. Be very certain of the bit you use so that you don't cause physical injury. Don't trust just anyone to advise you in these. Be absolutely sure the person is knowledgeable and is caring about the feelings of the animal.

The clothing you wear will depend upon the type of tack you're using. For exercising, training or just pleasure riding, a pair of jeans and comfortable loafers will do. Make sure you have a good sole and a heel. Sandals are a no, no for riding. They're dangerous around a barn for you might get stepped on or stub your toe. An enclosed shoe is always best.

Bare feet are a big round NO. Shorts are not a good idea unless you're only going to be up for a few minutes to show someone what to do. If the horse panics at something and runs into bushes or anything prickly, your legs can be injured. Also, the sweaty hair on a horse does not feel good on the legs.

One of the girls working for me decided to cool off a horse by walking him on a trail while she rode bare foot and in shorts. He stepped in a hole and threw her. She got scratched up and then had to walk home leading the horse. Often, when the teens had worked hard, I did let them ride bareback and bare foot as they rode into a pond and swam the horses. Both animal and riders enjoyed this immensely.

It is often a big temptation to buy very cheap tack or use someone's who is getting rid of it. A used saddle might not fit your horse's back as the saddle wears to the shape of another horse. Put yourself in the place of wearing someone's old shoes.

Correct care is a must for all tack. Never just drop a saddle on the ground. If it has to go on the ground, stand it up on the nose so that the bottom can get air. Put a long nail or a screw into the bottom of a clean aluminum can. This makes a good saddle rack until you can make a good wooden one. Also wash the bridle after each use and hang it up on a can or a spool.

Blankets and/or pads must be used on any and all saddles. Keep these clean and aired out to make them comfortable for the animal and to last longer.

The weight of the saddle should be evenly distributed and not rubbing on the back. Remember the kidneys are under the back of the saddle.

Helmets or hard hats should be worn by all new riders and riders training a horse. These should be worn regardless of what tack you're using.

The Western saddle is made much like the saddle of the Middle Ages and the old Spanish saddle. The older saddles had a deep seat with a high pommel (front or nose) and cantle (back) to support the rider. One of this type was also used for a war saddle. Because the horses were very active and the men were in the saddle for long periods of time, the deep seat was for comfort.

The Lippizan horses have been taught to perform in much the way of the old war horses in battle. I was fortunate to ride one once at the Army station in Washington, D.C.

As the Spanish conquistadors (cowboys) built tremendous herds of cattle and large ranches, they needed the deeper saddle for comfort because they were often all day in the saddle. Those who rode and guarded all night appreciated the deeper saddle to doze occasionally.

The Western saddle is primarily a working saddle. I have jumped in mine and do require my Western students to learn to jump. In the event they are on a trail and a tree has fallen across it, or they're in a mountain region, they may have to jump a stream or over an obstacle. I don't recommend that the average person make a jumping saddle out of a Western saddle; just be prepared for emergencies.

The horn, or nose, of a Western saddle is to hold a rope or working equipment, not to hold on to ride. In some instances one may be forced to grab leather (hold the horn) if a horse spooks or acts silly at the wrong time. Also, a well-trained cutting horse may shuck off (slide out from under a rider by stopping or turning quickly) when you're least expecting it and leave you hanging in mid air. One tried that on me and I joked that I left my finger prints (holds) on the cantle. I've never been thrown from a horse except when one fell with me.

The girth holds the saddle on just as belts hold trousers in place. The working Western saddle will have two girths. Old western riders often used tapaderos or curved protectors on the front of the stirrup to keep the cold winds from their feet and to protect their feet from thorny bushes. The strings on the back of the saddle are for tying on camping equipment, change of clothing or rain gear. I leave a hoof pick tied there all the time.

A decorative Western saddle for shows and parades can weigh close to two hundred pounds if there is silver on it. Place this with the weight of a rider and the poor horse is carrying a load.

Monty Foreman, a well-known rider and instructor as well as author and public speaker, has developed a flat type of Western saddle which permits quick dismounts.

Early military troops of Europe used a relatively flat saddle. Our own military men of the 1800s (War Between the States) used a similar saddle with only the tree covered. This left an opening down the middle of the saddle where it fitted over the spinal column of the horse. Heavy blankets and pads were needed to protect the horse's back.

I have one of these saddles (called a McClellan), with 1840 stamped on it. I also have a hand-tooled (handmade) Western side saddle made either in the late 1700s and not later than 1800. I donated both saddles to the Old West Museum in Cheyenne, Wyoming. A saddle maker told me that he thought the side saddle was made in or near Wyoming was the main reason I left them there. Also, the

Indians and whites were starting the museum together. I wanted to help.

I also had a bag made of horse hide that my maternal grandmother used as her doctor bag. She rode side saddle all over the mountain area of Virginia, Kentucky, Tennessee and North Carolina doctoring and helping people. Of course she had to use herbs and home remedies as there were no pharmacies. The bag had been handed down to her by her cousin who was one of the first U.S. Marshalls. He retired at the age of seventy something and she was just starting in her late twenties.

Grandmother Bolling-Stallard lived to a ripe old age and, in spite of her duties away from home, she had thirteen children. My mother was the youngest and sometimes rode with her mother helping to deliver babies and prepare the dead for burial.

The forward seat English saddle has a deep seat in the center with thick knee rolls to support the knee and hold the rider's point of balance when jumping. All purpose saddles are made of good leather and designed to be used for any type of work. It is good for daily work, jumping, dressage, and training. The knee roll is not thick, but is sufficient for cross-country work. The smooth flap, or fender, allows the rider to use the saddle for dressage.

Some saddles have a breastplate, or leather strap, going around the horse's chest to keep the saddle from slipping back. Some will have a crouper, or leather strap, under the tail to keep the saddle from slipping too far forward. You will not need these unless your horse has a conformation fault.

The park seat, or saddle seat, also has no knee roll. The pommel is cut back deeply to allow more neck action of the horse. Posting is behind the action and the weight of the rider is more in the stirrup than in the knee. Although when I post bare back, I have to use my knees.

Posting is rising up and down with the action of the horse. Always post on the outside of a circle such as a ring. When on a long ride and posting, change shoulders so as to not make the horse sore on one side. Rise up when the shoulder of the horse is going forward, sit when coming back. Make sure your motion is graceful so that you don't flap and plop on the poor horse's back and hurt him.

When buying tack, check for the grade of leather. Some are excellent, some are just good and some (as the Japanese) are poor, thin quality that does not hold up if it gets wet. The tree (base) of the saddle should be of really good quality. I prefer wood with steel reinforcements, but today there are more made of fiberglass and vinyl, which is good.

Again, the saddle to fit to the horse is most important. It should fit the horse's back as well as the requirements of the rider. The bridle is very important. It must fit the horse correctly and be comfortable. A poor fit will not only cause pain and discomfort, but will teach the horse to hate to work.

The bit fits across the bar of the mouth and over the tongue. The throat latch (called lash) fits loosely around the throat. It should fit so that an average fist will fit snugly when placed between the leather and the horse's throat. If it is too tight, it interferes with the horse's breathing and flexion.

The brow band keeps the bridle from slipping off backward. Most Western bridles do not have a brow band. They usually have an open section to fit over only one ear. It is just as comfortable on the horse if it is fitted properly. The head piece holds the cheek pieces so that they can support the bit. The nose band (cavesson) of an English bridle should fit halfway between the corners of the mouth and the cheek bone. It should be loose enough to allow the thumb to lie sideways under it.

The bit should be fitted so that there is just a slight wrinkle to the corners of the mouth. If it is too high or narrow, it will pinch the horse's lips and cause pain and often injury. If it is too low or too loose, it is of no value as a control.

If a curb chain is used, it should be flat and not pinching. When the horse is relaxed, you should be able to get one finger between the curb chain and the chin of the horse.

The reins attach to the bit. This is one means of communication that the rider uses with the horse. Any bit, in the wrong hands, can be painful and the horse will consider it a punishment.

Making a good mouth on a horse is important. This means to fit a bit properly and use soft but firm hands to guide and control the action of the horse. Even though my Cherokee was spirited and always ready to go, he could have been ridden with a soft string in his mouth. I never used a rough bit or hard hands on him or any horse.

Remember, the bridle is for communication and not for the rider to hold his or her weight on the horse.

When I start a new rider I like to lunge them on a bare back pad. This helps develop balance and builds their confidence. It also keeps the inexperienced person from pulling roughly on the mouth of the horse. I add saddle next and then the stirrups. Last of all the rider gets to hold the reins. The rider, hopefully, has learned natural aids for balance and for guiding the animal without causing pain.

Bridles should be washed and saddles wiped clean after each use. The girth should be cleaned and saddle blankets or pads shaken and left out to dry. Wash them as needed, but don't put off too long. All tack should be taken apart, cleaned and oiled about once a week.

Have sponges, terrycloth toweling, a good saddle soap, metal polish, dandy brush, cotton swabs (for tight or small places) glycerin or Vaseline, a bucket, a comfortable place to sit and old clothes for yourself. If not wearing old clothes, have a large apron. Do not use too much water and do not dry near heat. Wipe oils off well because some oils will burn the skin of the horse.

You don't need expensive items to keep your tack in shape. As I've said, vegetable or juice cans be used to hang bridles, barrels can be used to hold saddles or make a wooden rack. Don't just drop the saddle down and cause the leather to gradually break. Do not hang the bridle on a nail for it is too small and will eventually cause the leather to break. Place a clean blanket over the items to keep dust and dirt off them.

IMPORTANT

Before beginning the chapter on lunging, driving and riding, I must call attention to some important facts. For the health and safety of the young animal, never make the training sessions too long or too demanding. Fifteen minutes at a time is sufficient. Gradually add time and training techniques. As the animal matures and gains experience, the time can be developed.

I never mount a horse before two years of age, then with a lightweight person. I never start serious jumping or serious Western training until three years of age.

When a person is lunging or driving an animal, it is very important to pay attention and not wrap lunge lines around the hands or any parts of your body. Stay alert and do not drop the line where it can wrap around the ankle or break a leg.

Training should NEVER be in the hands of an inexperienced person unless there is supervision with a knowledgeable person present. It is easier (and the animal is happier) to train correctly at first than to break bad habits and retrain. I hate like the dickens to try to retrain someone's bad training.

Please do not make the mistake of feeling that you can train or give riding lessons just because you have read a book or had a handful of lessons. Learn as much as you can from everyone you meet and learn from your own experiences.

Just as an interesting addition, the Friesian horse and the large Shire were two of the big horses used by the knights with all that heavy armor. The Friesian is a beautiful, graceful animal from Friesland which is just north of the Netherlands. As a rule they are gentle and eager to please with a very easy gait. They are usually coal black.

The Shire (the love of my life) is the largest of the draft horses and comes mostly from England. They can grow as high as twenty-two hands and are truly "a gentle giant". The largest one on record weighed three thousand three hundred pounds.

LUNGING AND DRIVING

Lunging is a most important part of a horse's education in training and keeping in shape. It is a means of communication between horse and handler. This can be a great asset, however if lunging is not done correctly, it can be the worst thing a person can do to a horse.

I will only discuss the means by which I work with a horse as each trainer has his or her own methods.

Starting with a foal, I place a soft, cloth halter on him. A gentle voice and kind words will make a little fellow more willing to be handled and to learn. I gently lead him along and say, "come"; then he gets a lot of hugs and praise. Handle with care and patience to avoid scaring him and to avoid injuring soft, tender joints that have not matured.

Use terrycloth and wipe him all over daily while talking, singing and praising him. After a few months, I place one hand behind his rump and another on his chest and say, "walk"... I give a lot of praise and petting. Should he pull back in confusion or fright, I say, "ease, easy." The dam is, of course, beside him all the time. If she has been trained properly she might even nicker and encourage him. If he runs off a few steps or jumps around, I don't chase him. I just wait until he is in position again and start over. Handle him on both sides so he will be prepared to be handled all over.

Sometimes a young horse gets too frisky to be led by hands and arms. Then you will need a "come along". This is a soft rope that is placed under the rump and pulled through the under side of the halter. I have taken sheets or soft blankets, ripped them into three pieces, and braided a soft rope for myself. When you want him to stop and stand say, "stand ho." No and ho sound so much alike you'll have to distinguish between them. Or say "no, no" twice.

WHEN TRAINING, ONLY ONE PERSON SHOULD DO THE TALKING. TOO MANY VOICES WILL BE CONFUSING.

Okay, you're saying, "That's silly. Just start asking him to do what you want him to do." Sure, I take longer than most trainers to work, but I get results without fighting and build trust and confidence. Laugh if you will, but my horses love me. I've seen the goofy, glazed look in their eyes when they look at me. Rewards mean less pressure and more praise.

At about a month of age, I stand him against his mother (or another SILENT person) and gently lift each foot. I use two fingers to tap on the bottom of the hoof and get him ready for the farrier to work with him. Don't try to stand him out in the open yet because he might fall and be frightened.

The horse does not have a big brain, but he does have a phenomenal memory. It is important that his memories are good ones. Even when working with an older horse that's new to you, work patiently and start from scratch because you don't know what kind of training he has had.

At two months of age most of them are ready for a leather halter. They can be led by a lead rope. By now he should know "come", "walk" and "stand ho". I also use any special call, whistle or whatever that I'm going to be using to call him in from the field. Let him know this means love and sometimes a snack. I use the crunchy pieces made from apples or carrots.

If one is slow in responding, turn him out with an older or well trained horse. When you whistle or call, the older one will respond and the other one will learn, just as children learn from copying us.

NEVER lunge a foal before one year of age. Through the first year, joints and muscles need time to develop, strengthen and set. Shoulders, hips and hocks can be damaged permanently by lunging too early.

During the first lunging trainings, two people are more satisfactory. One to lead on the outside of the circle, WITHOUT SPEAKING, and one to be inside the circle directing. Stand about even with the horse where your foot and stirrup will be. Always work him in both directions to avoid soreness or injury to one side. The lunge line is attached to the ring in the halter.

Walk should be just one word. Trot starts out with a higher note at the beginning of the word "TER ot". Canter will be soft, starting "Can TER".

To reverse, make sure he turns away from you. I don't ask mine to canter until they are about fifteen months of age. I know they run and play in the field, but this is restricted work. When you ask for "stand ho", do not allow them to turn and look at you. They must stay in the circle position. While working with a yearling make your circles large with short sessions. After each lesson, give a good rub-down with lots of praise.

A lunge whip can be used for direction, NOT to hit the horse. Sometimes snapping the end of the lunge line will be enough. The noise alone is sufficient to keep their attention.

At about eighteen months of age, I place the surcingle on him for driving. Not that I expect to drive him --- or I might, but to prepare him for being directed by a rider through the reins. The surcingle is a simple form that can be made at home. I use a four inch wide piece of canvas belt that will fasten around the barrel of the horse, firmly but not too tight. This will also prepare him for the girth of the saddle. I sew curtain rings on each side about three inches apart. Two thirty-foot ropes fit from the halter (or bridle) back through the reins and to the handler. In this manner the horse can be taught to rein without a load on his back. He needs to only think about one part of training at a time.

When teaching him to turn, make sure the whole body turns and not just his neck and head. His neck should be flexible, but not on these turns. Keep the lines straight, but stay back to keep from being kicked. Even a mild-mannered animal can object to these lines the first time. Keep the lines along with the place where your feet and stirrups will be. If it's too high, you might be teaching him to rear, which can be dangerous. If too low, he will tuck his nose down too much and not have a good head set. Do not wrap the lines around your hand because he might bolt and try to run. You don't want to be pulled over and dragged.

During the first couple of times driving, it is wise to have someone (silently) walk on the outside near his head just for comfort. The handler says "walk" and lets some pressure off the lines. Work in both directions.

If turning left, gently pull the left rein and lay the right line against the body of the horse. Turn the whole body. If turning right, pull gently on the right rein and lay the left line against the body. Don't snap the line against the body. It will panic him.

When he is working well with halter and bridle, in both directions, I then use a bare back pad and tie about a twenty-five pound weight on the pad. The next week I make that a fifty pound weight. Then comes the saddle. Let him see it and smell it first. Gently lay it up near the base of the neck and slide back into place along with the growth of the hair.

At about a year of age, I lay about six or eight poles flat on the ground (called cavallettis) so that he learns to place his feet correctly and balance himself. I work in both directions for just a few minutes. I come back to it later for a few more minutes. After about four or five months of this, I lay about five poles on the ground and place bricks, or something low, under the sixth pole. He will step a little higher, but will not jump. I do this even for horses that I'm training Western.

As he matures I raise the height of the last pole, not to jump, just to place his feet more carefully. After a couple of months, I lay two poles about six inches apart at the higher level to teach him to stretch his body instead of scrambling and lunging.

Even well-trained horses need to be taken back through the basics about once a year to relax them and keep their confidence.

When I observe a horse rushing, sweating, panting and getting excited I know that ninety-nine percent of the time his training has been rushed and he's feeling insecure.

Training a horse in a patient manner assures me that he won't buck or fight. Oh, on a cold morning he may jump around a little or on a beautiful spring day he may dance and prance, but he's felling good and cheerful, not fighting.

Patient training means that when you place a saddle on him at two years old, he trusts you and will want to please. After he's accustomed to the saddle on a lunge line, then I add light weight and finally a light person.

Cones can be placed to ride a figure eight or in a straight line to do in and outs. I teach all Western and English horses to open rein and neck rein. This increases suppleness and confidence. It can rest the English horse on a long trail ride.

Your training methods, length of time for each lesson, and how much is taught at once, will depend upon the personality and maturity of the horse.

BACKING

Backing is not a natural movement for the horse. This is an important part of the training though, so be very careful you don't injure or cripple the horse. The head and neck are supported by the front legs. When the weight of the head shifts, the horse will transfer its weight on the front leg in the direction the head is turning.

I suggest being against a fence with a rope or temporary fence as another side. Stand at the shoulder facing backwards. Never stand in front in the event that the horse gets confused and rears up.

Look to see which front foot is forward. That's the one you want him to move back. Hold the lead rope close under the chin of the horse. If the right front foot is farther forward, then slightly turn the head to the left over the foot that is behind. Put pressure, with your hand or a training devise, on the shoulder or the chest. Say "back" until he moves, then praise him. Pressure on the shoulder is better because later the leg aids will take the place of this.

Keep doing this from one side to the other until he takes more than one step. Give lots of praise. When you're in the saddle, the bit pressure and leg pressure are the only aids you need. TIME AND PATIENCE.

If he shakes his head and tries to rear, step to one side and calm him. Don't make this training session too long. Remember, it's unnatural and stressful for him. When you're finally on his back, be careful to not get the reins high or he'll think he has to rear.

Some people with little experience, or knowledge, think it's smart to make him rear. This only shows the inability of the rider to be a responsible owner and rider.

I've seen some people twist in the saddle and throw themselves backward in their seat and pull hard on the reins. This only punishes the horse.

Please don't start the Western horse on a rollback until the horse can back and work without nervous movements. Jerking hard on the horse's mouth and throwing your body around is NOT a rollback. Please, please get professional help with this or risk crippling your horse for life.

The rider's seat (balance) is vitally important. Take lessons so that you're a rider and not a passenger. The horse is a living, breathing being with feelings and will serve you faithfully.

TACKING UP

This means to place the saddle and bridle on the horse. First tie the horse in a safe place using a slip knot. Groom carefully so that dirt is not under the saddle rubbing and causing an irritation. Always check the feet. Make sure the bridle is clean and fitting properly. Wipe the eyes, nose and ears, as well as under the tail, private parts and elbow with a clean cloth. Do you need a fly spray?

DO NOT RIDE AS SOON AS THE HORSE HAS EATEN. If he is recuperating from an injury, or has been standing for awhile, never work more than half an hour. Start slowly; not running and cowboying.

Is the girth clean and free of dried hair or sweat? Is your pad or blanket clean and has it been well aired? Place the pad or blanket high on the withers and slide it down with the way the hair is growing. Gently lift the saddle on the back, remembering the kidneys are under the back of the saddle. Fasten the girth, but not tight.

If you are going on a long ride, or plan to be tacked up a long time, you will probably want to leave the halter on under the bridle. In this way, when you stop for a while, you can take off the bridle to allow his mouth to rest and tie him by the halter. Also, when you stop and get off for any reason, loosen the girth, but don't forget to tighten it again before you mount.

One February, our riding group was in the George Washington Day parade in Arlington, Virginia. I was riding side saddle on my Morgan mare and dressed in a full colonial-style skirt with a white, ruffled blouse. I had a beautician make a fall matching my hair so that I had a long fall of hair over one shoulder. I wore my own riding britches under the skirt.

I had not tightened the girth before the parade. Then we were given the signal to fall in the parade before we expected it. My friend's father came along and literally threw me up on the horse. None of us thought to tighten the girth. Well along the street my horse was prancing and nodding her head from side to side as if she were acknowledging the people clapping. Suddenly my girth slipped and I landed on the street with the saddle hanging under the poor mare's belly. She stopped immediately. My skirt flew up and I was sure glad I had on the full riding gear under my skirt. My husband came along and took the saddle while I jumped up bareback and finished the parade.

Coming home, always walk back to the stable. Never, ever allow your horse to get in the habit of running home. They know the food and their buddies are there and will run right into the back. You could get a bad head wound on the door top or even break your neck. It isn't good for the horse.

Walk carefully to cool off. Loosen the girth and allow air to flow under the saddle. This will prevent cramps in the back muscles. I was on an endurance ride and there were veterinarian checks every few miles. One woman rushed up, threw off her horse's saddle and he immediately screamed and went down. His back was in cramps and he was in agony. The vet had to give him a shot to calm him down and later a gentle back massage. That silly woman wanted to know how soon she could saddle up and catch up with the others. She was told to go home and have her veterinarian check the animal again. He was not to be ridden for at least a week.

When you take off the bridle, rub behind the ears and around the mouth to help circulation. Be sure he is cooled down and had a good brisk brushing before turning him loose. Now he can have water and hay. If it is cold weather, I hope you have a blanket to put on him. Treat him as you would want to be treated.

Some of this takes time, but once you get into a routine, it will not seem too long. It's worth all the time and effort to own a horse.

Now wash the bridle and hang it properly. Wipe the saddle and lay or hang it where it won't be broken or scratched. Leave the pads and blankets out to air unless it's time for them to be washed. Put all your grooming equipment in proper places so that it will be handy the next time you need it.

MOUNTING AND EXERCISING

Mounting means how you get up on your horse… See the items on Tacking Up to be sure you're prepared to ride.

Stand on the near side (left side) of the horse with your left shoulder near his while you're facing backwards. Gather the reins with equal length. Do not pull back on them or the horse might back up or rear. Use a mounting block if you are too short to mount or if you're physically unable to mount in the traditional way.

In rare occasions, a horse might try to bite your rear as you try to mount. If this happens, just shorten the off (right) rein a tiny bit so he can't turn his head to bite you.

The mane has no nerve endings so feel free to pull up by the mane if you need to. It is much better if you learn to balance on one foot and bounce up.

Take the left stirrup in your right hand and turn it to face you. Place your left toe on the iron or wood of the stirrup. Place your right hand on the opposite side of the saddle to push down as you mount so that you're not pulling your complete weight on the horse's side. Stand up in the left stirrup and raise your right leg lowering it gently on the other side so that you don't kick the horse. Lower yourself gently in the saddle so that you don't jar and hurt his back. Animals have backaches, too.

Do you know why we mount on the left side? During the middle ages, when knights rode, a sword was always on the left side of the body. If he had mounted on the right side of the animal, then when he lifted his left leg, the sword would have banged on the horse. Therefore, he mounted on the left so that the sword hung straight down.

Sit in the lowest part of the saddle. Adjust your stirrups by leaving your leg hanging straight down. The stirrup should be just at the bottom of your ankle bone. Your foot should rest in the stirrup so that the iron, or wood, is across the ball of the foot with the big toe touching the inside of the stirrup. The heel should be slightly down. The knees will be bent just slightly for comfort.

Pick up the reins making sure both are straight with even pressure. With English reins, you will hold the reins in your hand with your palms turned toward you. Allow the loose end of the rein to hang over your right hand and to the right side. Your hand should be just tight enough to apply pressure to give directions, but not to be harsh.

Your little finger can exert fifty pounds of pressure. Be careful. Your arm should be relaxed with your elbow slightly bent and near the body. The thumbs will be turned up and slightly in. The wrist should be relaxed. When directing by the reins, your arms will move slightly back and forth, not twisting your wrist and jerking.

Reins held high make it impossible to make good contact with the animal. Also, he might be encouraged to rear, shake his head or fight. Reins held too low put too much pressure on the bit and mouth. With low reins, the rider has a tendency to lean forward and be thrown off balance. AS THE HEAD GOES, SO GOES THE BODY. Want to come off over the horse's head?

A young or green Western horse will be trained with a rein in each hand. Otherwise take both reins in the hand in which you do not use to write. The position of your free arm is where riding instructors disagree. Some say carry the free arm across your waist line. Some say allow the arm to remain in a natural position hanging by the side.

I use the theory of the old cowboys. A worker, on the range, would get mighty tired holding his arm up. He rode with his arm relaxed and ready to throw a rope or shoot a gun. I have seen too many Western riders in horse shows holding the arm across their middle. If the person is an inexperienced rider, or gets tired, or the horse has a rough gait, they end up by making a fist and holding tight across themselves as if they have severe cramps. RELAX. The elbow should not stick out like a bird trying its wings.

Turning the Western horse is also a common disagreement. I teach the horse to turn the whole body. If I want him to turn right, I lay the reins against the left side of the neck and place my right heel slightly back to cue him to turn his rump away from my heel. If I want a left turn, I lay the reins against the right side of the neck and place my left heel back slightly to get his rump to turn away from my heel.

Everyone should take Equitation lessons. Equitation means how the rider sits and communicates with the horse. The rider will be safer and so will the horse.

Exercises are good for a number of reasons. They help build natural balance and give confidence... They help a rider move with more grace and less effort so as to have a more enjoyable ride for both horse and rider.

I once took a class of eleven young women who were in their middle twenties to late thirties. They came to me and said they wanted to exercise, although a few admitted being afraid. They were amused at themselves, but supportive and encouraged each other. They did have a lot of fun and hated to stop. They developed better eating habits, but most importantly they had healthy, therapeutic riding. I'm not a nutritionist, but I did recommend good meal planning both at home and when eating out. For years afterward we met once a month for lunch and to share news of ourselves and our families.

Let me urge you not to take these exercises alone or on a young, green horse. At first you should have someone to either walk beside you or ride a calm, gentle horse beside you. Do all of these at a walk before you try a trot or canter. Believe it or not, most of them are easier at a canter than a trot. They are good for both English and Western riders. Set a regular schedule and stick to it.

WESTERN

PARK or SADDLE SEAT

ENGLISH

EXERCISES

When riding, keep your heels tilted down to keep yourself from falling forward. I take a rider's foot out of the stirrup and hang a loose stirrup on the toes. They have to keep the toes up to keep from dropping the stirrup. I sometimes use a thirty-two ounce plastic glass.

Stand on the ground facing another person. Place your hands in their hands and stand naturally. Ask them to pull you and they can pull you forward. Stand slightly on your toes and you'll go over much quicker. Stand with your heel firmly down and the toes slightly up and the knees bent just a little. It will be next to impossible for them to pull you over. The point I'm making is that your heels work as a brake in the air. Your head must be upright; shoulders and back as straight as possible without being uncomfortable.

Keeping the heels down and the legs in correct position, sit well in the saddle without squeezing your legs. Let your weight fall in your thighs. Leaning from the waist, touch the horse's left ear with your right hand. Straighten up from the waist. Lean to touch the horse's right ear with your left hand. At first only do these exercises three times. Each day add one until you are doing ten each.

Put your arms straight our to the side, move from the waist as far to the left as you can and then to the right. Again work up to ten. Keeping the arms straight out, touch the horse's head with one hand and then reach as far back as you can to touch the rump with the other hand. Movements are all from the waist with the stomach as flat as possible.

Hold one leg out to the side and slowly circle it. Then bend the knee and straighten the leg. Do the same with the other leg.

As you advance, bend forward from the waist to put your face near the horse's neck. (Be careful that he doesn't throw his head back and hit you). Then lean as far back as you can. Lay on the rump if possible. Rise up to a sitting position using only the thigh muscles. Don't squeeze the legs.

Bend the elbows and keep them bent. Push the arm as far forward as possible and then as far back as possible.

Roll each ankle one at a time in a circle in each direction. Using thigh muscles, lean over to touch your left foot with the right hand and then your right foot with the left hand. These are only a few with which I work.

As you advance more, stand in the stirrups keeping the heels slightly down and the toes up. Balance standing while the horse walks. DON'T PULL ON THE REINS. Later you can trot and canter while standing. Please, please have someone beside you.

A trip around the world is fun for very advanced riders. Do not try it alone in the event the horse panics and moves. Remove your feet from the stirrups. Put your leg over the horse without touching him, and move to the side. Move to the back facing backward. Still without touching the horse, move around until you are on the other side and then finally back in place.

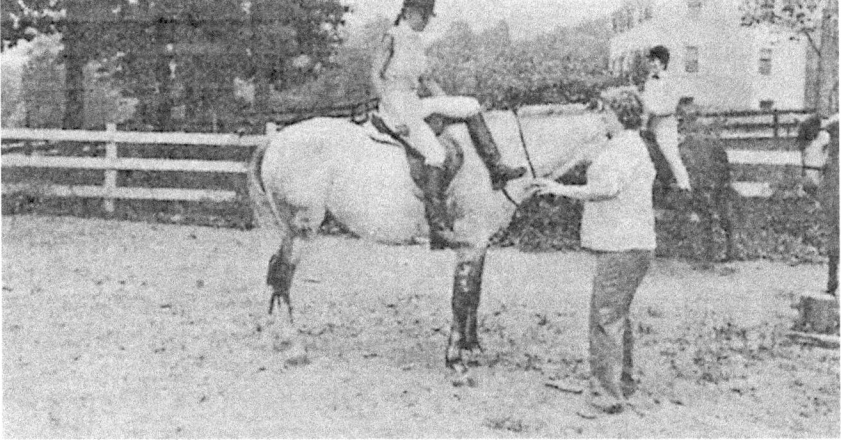

Starting the trip around the world

DISMOUNTING AND EMERGENCY DISMOUNTING

Dismounting is getting off the horse without kicking him. Stand in the left stirrup and lift the right leg over the horse's back. There are two ways to dismount. Some take out the left foot and drop to the ground. Some step down with the right foot and then remove the left. Make sure your foot isn't caught in the stirrup. Keep the reins in your hand.

Loosen the girth and walk the horse to cool him. Then remove tack, brush the horse, clean the tack and put everything in its place. Don't forget to check the feet. Then give water and hay.

EMERGENCY DISMOUNTING

Let's hope and pray you won't have to do this, but it's good to know. It's one of the first things I teach. Always stay with the horse if possible.

If a horse panics and tries to run or fight, run him in circles, slowing down gradually and making smaller circles. Then he'll really need cooling down.

If you're too afraid to do this, or he won't respond, then fold your arms across your chest to protect your chest. Take your feet out of the stirrups. Jump off to one side, rounding your shoulders, bending your knees, and rolling when you hit the ground.

I was horrified when I heard a girl at the 4-H show telling a friend, "Wrap your arms around the horse's neck and roll off." The forward motion of the horse would pull you under the horse and you would have a very serious injury or be killed.

The idea of an emergency dismount is to get safely away from the horse. I recommend that, before you do this on a horse, you practice dropping and rolling on a mat or something soft until you get the idea. Learn to relax your knees and ankles to minimize strains and breaks.

Remember, this is only in emergency situations. Stay with your horse when possible and keep the reins in your hands.

The following are pictures of my friend, Dee Ford, who lost her life to cancer. This wonderful lady was active to the end without complaining. She was the first to give a word of encouragement to others and was always smiling. I did not get pictures of her crossing her arms and rolling. She first placed her hands on the horse's neck, brought her legs over safely without kicking the horse and dropped. As she dropped she crossed her arms over her chest, bent her knees and rolled. As much as we love our animals, they can be replaced ---- humans can't.

MARKINGS AND COLORS

STAR	A light colored space on the forehead
SNIP	A light colored space on the nose
STRIPE	A narrow light colored strip down the center of the face
BLAZE	A wider light colored stripe down the center of the face
BALD	Most of the face light colored
STOCKINGS	White up to the hocks or knees (on the front, forelegs - on the back, aft legs)
SOCKS	A white area half-way up the leg.
PASTERN	Just the pastern area showing white
HALF ASTERN	Half of the pastern showing white
CORONET	Just a white circle around the coronet

Sioux Dallas

STAR

SNIP

STRIPE

BLAZE

BALD

STAR & STRIPE

STAR & BLAZE

STAR, STRIPE & SNIP

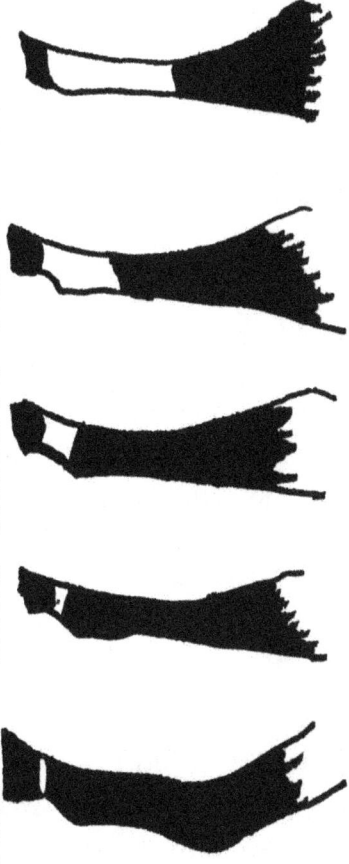

STOCKINGS

SOCKS

PASTERN

HALF PASTERN

CORONET

133

ALBINO - Colorless, whitish hair, pink skin and usually blue eyes

APPALOOSA - Spotted markings. The blanket is a white area on the rump with round or elongated spots. The Leopard is all white with dark spots. Sometimes the spots are so dark they look purple in the sun. The Snowflake is dark with spots and splashes of white. The Marbleized is a combination of dark and light, spots, splashes, etc. Blur Roan is white with dark tips and dots on hair, making it look as if pepper has been sprinkled on the horse. Red Roan or Strawberry Roan is white with red or reddish-brown tips and spots. Spots on the Appaloosa stand out and can be felt above the hair. A true Appaloosa will have mottled coloring around the eyes, nostrils, lips and genitals. The hoof is often striped.

BAY - Shades of brown or reddish brown. The points are black. (Points are mane and tail.) A blood-red bay is a beautiful deep deep red with dark points. Mealy bays show light coloring around the muzzle; sometimes called mule mouth. These are not desirable for show purposes.

BLACK - Hair and skin are black. Any markings will be white. Jet blacks shine like polished metal. Sunburned or rusty blacks are less desirable. A foal that will mature to black is often mouse grey or charcoal at birth.

BROWN - Dark brown or nearly black with brown or black points. Seal brown is often mistaken for black at a distance. Has tan on the muzzle and sometimes on the inner thigh.

BUCKSKIN - A muddy cream or tan color with black points.

CHESTNUT - A light golden red or a deep reddish brown with points of the same color. The light golden red will often have points of blond-red coloring.

CLAYBANK – A deep golden cream coloring with points a shade darker.

CREAM - More like a diluted shade of chestnut. Darker creams will show a little pigment in the skin while lighter creams might be pink-skinned with a white mane. The really pale creams are sometimes called albinos, however a true albino has no pigment in hair, skin or eyes.

DUN - Creamy or muddy shades of brown. Some are called mouse or smokey dun. They have black points and often have a dark strip down the center of the back much like the Jerusalem donkey. A Zebra dun will have stripes like a zebra on its legs.

GREY - Varies from a dark steel grey to almost white. As a grey get older, they often lighten in color. Usually born black or charcoal, and turn to grey as they shed baby hairs.

Points may be black or a shade lighter than the rest of the body. Greys and whites are more susceptible to sunburn.

GRULLO - Difficult to truly describe without looking at one. They are a mixture of grayish brown and black with dark points. Often has a dorsal stripe (down the center of the back).

PAINT - The Overo paint generally has no white between the withers and the tail. Irregular markings. The Tobiano paint will have white on the back with a solid colored head. Regular, distinct, oval markings. Often solid coloring on the chest will resemble a shield.

PALOMINO - Varies from light gold to reddish gold with light colored points. Sometimes mistaken for a cream. Must have dark skin and dark eyes.

PINTO - Often called a spotted pony. Mutation in pigment cause odd colorings. One is called a calico. A skewbald is white with patches of red or brown or tan. A piebald is white with patches of black. The patches can be anywhere and any shape on the body.

SORREL - A ginger-red coloring with the same shade of points or slightly darker points. Sometimes mistaken for a dark chestnut.

WHITE - One true form of white is conditioned by a dominant gene which gives pure white hair. Eyes and skin are dark. No true breeding form has been found.

DEFINITIONS

AFT - The rear part of a horse.

FORE - The front part of a horse.

NEAR - The left side of a horse.

OFF - The right side of a horse.

CHESTNUT - A horny growth on the inside of the leg.

CORNET - The line between the hoof and the leg.

ERGOT - A horny growth at the base of the pastern.

GET - Offspring (children). For example, he is the get of Top Deck.

HANDS - A horse is measured in hands. One hand is four inches.

FOAL - Any newborn horse.

COLT - A male foal.

FILLY - A female foal.

SUCKLING - A nursing foal.

WEANLING - One who has just been weaned.

SIRE - The father of the horse.

DAM - The mother of the horse.

STALLION - A grown male ready for breeding.

MARE - A grown female ready for breeding.

CAST or CASTE - A horse will sometimes roll for pleasure or in pain and will get stuck in that position, on the back or side against a fence, wall, etc. He might just lie there getting stiff and sore and crowding his intestines. Or he might fight to get up and cause serious injury. A veterinarian will give him a shot to calm him. Do not feed or water immediately or he might colic due to stress.

BLOOD HORSE - A Thoroughbred with both sire and dam registered in the General Stud Book. A half-breed has one Thoroughbred parent and another of a registered breed.

GRADE HORSE - Mixed breed or uncertain breeding.

HOT BLOODS - Mostly Eastern breeds such as Arabs, Akhal-teke or Barbs. The modern Thoroughbred, Arab, Anglo-Arab and Standardbred are hot bloods.

WARM BLOODS - Mostly sport horses; strong, useful horses. Crossed with hot bloods. These include the Friesian, Hanoverian, Lipizzaner, and hunters.

COLD BLOODED - Are the heavier horses such as the draft animals. Most of them are huge, heavily-muscled with coarse joints and not particularly fast. Remember, horses are mammals and all of them are "blooded".

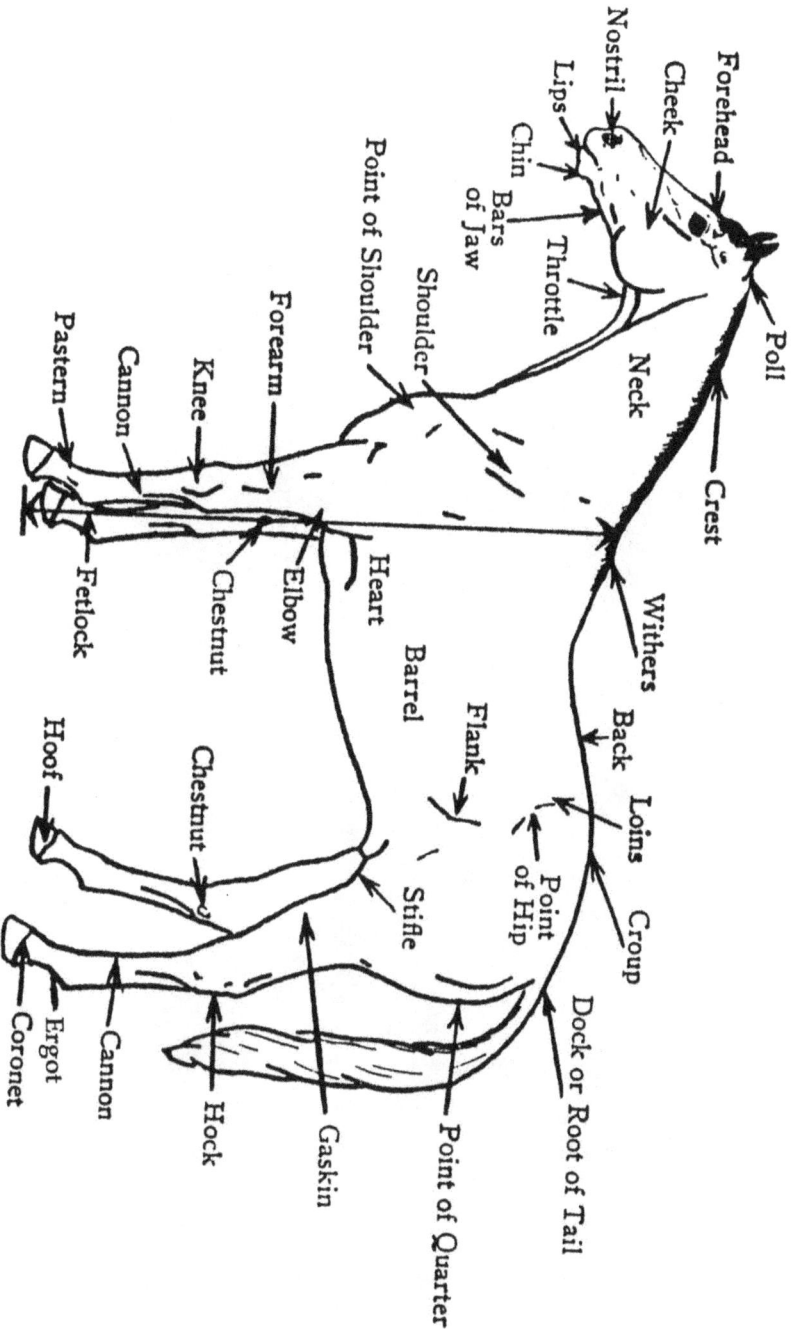

Forehead
Poll
Cheek
Nostril
Lips
Chin
Bars of Jaw
Throttle
Crest
Neck
Point of Shoulder
Shoulder
Withers
Back
Loins
Croup
Forearm
Knee
Cannon
Pastern
Fetlock
Chestnut
Elbow
Heart
Barrel
Flank
Point of Hip
Dock or Root of Tail
Hoof
Chestnut
Stifle
Hock
Gaskin
Point of Quarter
Coronet
Ergot
Cannon

Picture of Sioux Dallas on a camel
Sioux's Special "Horse"

ON THE BIT STORIES

For over thirty years I wrote a weekly column in several newspapers which I called "On the Bit" by Sioux Dallas. I would like to share two of those with you.

May, 1993

As the golden noonday sun gave a final benediction, Cherokee Challenge was laid quietly to rest under his favorite shade tree, on Saturday, the day before Easter.

He was foaled on June 17, 1962 by Top Deck out of Miss Night Bar. This lively youngster was the great-grandson of Man O'War. He had the old man's coloring and love and skill of running.

Cherokee spoiled me for training and working with other horses because he was so willing and quick to learn. An honest horse with a deep heart, he became my friend, my confidant and my love. People told me they knew he loved me because when he looked at me his eyes would get a glazed look and he had a "loopy" expression on his face. He made me a better rider because he demanded it. A people lover and very gentle, he became quite excited and eager to work when under saddle. I rode him both English and Western, but he refused the side saddle. It took a stout-hearted rider to stay with the strong, determined horse on a hunt or when approaching a jump. One had better be ready because he was going over.

Nearing four years of age he was ready for serious jumping. For several years we galloped joyfully over the Virginia countryside in the hunts. It sometimes was disconcerting to be galloping toward a jump, or over a stream, to have Cherokee come to a sharp halt because he wanted to watch birds or butterflies or smell a patch of wild flowers.

He went willing and trustingly wherever he was led or directed. Dozens of blue ribbons (and others), trophies and prizes were earned by him under both English and Western saddle.

Cherokee loved to have his rider sing, especially when his name was placed in the song. He loved to snack on carrots, apples and rosebuds.

His love of music showed in his performance in musical rides and dressage. I taught square dancing on horseback (the horses do the dancing) and he quickly learned what part of the music meant to change a step.

On sunny winter days we would lie in the field just talking and sharing apple treats. I would lie against his stomach with my head on his shoulder while he dozed or listened and put in an occasional nicker.

At the age of sixteen and seventeen, he participated successfully in the Old Dominion (Virginia) Endurance Rides. His personality drew people to him wherever he went. During parades people were yelling, "Hello, Cherokee." He had a special place in his heart for anything small, children or animals. He enjoyed being in parades as much as he did the two television movies he was in.

I always taught in the summer Bible School at the church. We would have a western day and learn how our ancestors worshipped. I took Cherokee twice for the children to see. The first time I took him my husband was holding him and I had my back to him while talking a kindergarten teacher. She gasped and pushed against me to get by me. I turned around and the tiny tots were crawling under his stomach and reaching up to touch him and hanging on to his legs. He stood very still and just nickered.

I can find no Biblical reference of animals in Heaven. I can visualize Cherokee running happily and certainly where there would be music. As I look at the sky and see lovely red coloring with wisps of clouds, I will see Cherokee running free with his beautiful red-gold mane and tail streaming out with the look of eagles in his eyes.

Old friend, you were therapy for me when I was in pain and gave me thousands of happy hours. You gave pleasure to my daughter and husband and many, many friends. The pain in your injured foot broke my heart and I couldn't stand to see you in pain knowing how much you loved to run and jump. The veterinarian offered to amputate your foot and make a prosthesis for you. I said "No, thank you" because he loved to be active. With many tears I had to let you go. God blessed me with you. There will never be another one like you. So long, old friend, so long.

The second one that I wrote another week is true and funny:

There have been many fantastic, outrageous and true stories about "horse traders". Some of them are hilarious and some will make the listener angry enough to want to get involved.

There was a funny happening around 1872. One way that an Indian proved his value was by the number of horses he owned. Old Chief Howlish-Wampo was no exception. He prided himself on being rich in horse ownership.

The main form of recreation among the Umatilla Indians was to race, either foot races or horse races. There were many bets made -- and lost. The pale faces in the vicinity got wind of the races and that the Umatilla had many fine horses. Some of the whites sent word that they would like to race their horses against the Indian mounts. The old chief sent word that he would not agree to race his horses without a thousand dollar bet. Some of the Indians backed their chief until there was a twenty thousand dollar bet on their part.

The whites, who lived nearby, were wise to the old chief's tricks. They knew he would have a brave ride a scrawny horse up and, at the last minute, he would bring out this beautiful, strong horse. Foolish bettors would think they had a perfect chance of making a lot of money. The whites got together to match the bet, but finally agreed to give up their horses if they lost.

Sure enough, just as the race finally lined up to go, a brave pranced out on a strong, beautiful Appaloosa. That Appaloosa would be a quarter of a mile ahead before the other horses even got started. The old chief was even richer, and he did share with the braves who helped him.

Land began to open for settlement and people moved in who were not acquainted with the Umatilla Indians and their tricky chief. Even the whites sat back and enjoyed seeing these arrogant newcomers get "taken".

Naturally word traveled due to the progress of transportation by water and also the fact that people were not afraid to travel in Indian territory as much.

An Irishman, who was very proud of his horses, heard of the chief's bet. This man, from the green sod, had a heavy Irish hunter who was very fast in the hunt field. He had won several races on his own. He had even raced in the gold mining area around Boise and had won. He sent word that he would take the chief's bet. The story was the same. With a heavy heart he had to leave his precious horse behind.

Several months later a Frenchman decided he was too smart to be tricked by these Indians. He brought several good horses with him, but kept a real beauty hidden. At the last minute he trotted out this horse of his, but the Indians did the same and again the Indians won. They did give him a scrawny pony to get home on.

A gold miner decided that he would enter this bet. He and his buddy sneaked in after dark and stole the beautiful Appaloosa. They took turns running him all night until he was hanging his head and trembling.

He even told the other miners what he was doing and they gleefully bet thinking they had a sure thing.

He was grinning widely when the poor tired horse was lined up with his horse to race. His grin changed when the tired horse was led off and a big, strong, beautiful Appaloosa was placed in line.

Naturally the Indians won. The chief felt sorry for him when he saw that the other miners were ready to beat the man up for causing them to lose their money. He told him to take his horse and leave and the next time he felt like stealing a horse, be sure it was the one he meant it to be.

By this time the old chief had over two thousand horses of his own, and thousands of dollars in the white man's bank. He was rich in many ways, but he was richest in his sense of humor.

TRAILERING

TRAINING TO LOAD ON A TRAILER

THE FIRST WAY IS ONE ROPE BY
YOURSELF. THE SECOND WAY IS
TWO ROPES WITH AN ASSISTANT.

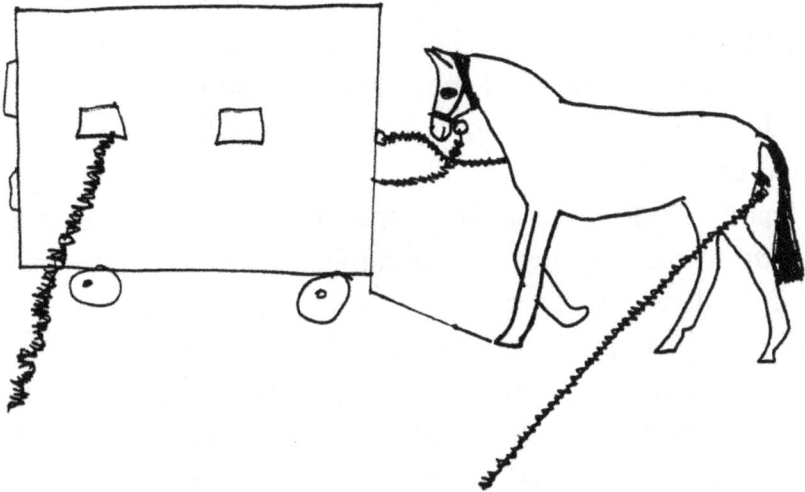

Let me explain why I am reluctant to tie a horse in a trailer when traveling. One warm day in late fall, my husband and I had been invited to go with a group for a pleasure ride and have refreshments later at a member's home.

At that time, I did not own a trailer, so one of the men insisted that I use his two-horse trailer for my horses. I did not know that he had relined the brakes himself without knowledge of doing the work.

We were traveling on a four lane highway with the lanes separated by a low bank. Suddenly a wheel locked on the trailer throwing the car out of control. We ended up on the bank and facing on-coming traffic. Fortunately other drivers saw my problem and had stopped. I had felt a jerk but did not know what had happened until I got out.

With shaking legs I got out thinking first of my horses. With heart in my throat I saw the front of the trailer up in the air and the back flat on the ground. I saw my two horses lying on the road behind me. Trying to be calm, I gave the whistle I always gave to call them and they got up and trotted up to me.

Thank God I had trained my horses. Cherokee trotted right up to me "talking" as he came. Behind him was Penny Ante, a dear twenty-three-year-old Morgan mare. I had taught my husband to ride on her. Both horses were wearing light blankets and neither had been tied. They had been thrown clear through the fiberglass roof and onto the road.

My veterinarian had been ready to go with the group but he left immediately and came when I called him. The blankets were torn in places and there was a tiny cut on the back leg of each horse, but otherwise they were fine. He gave them each a tranquilizer shot and used his car phone to call someone to come get me and take us back home. He praised me for not tying in this incident or they could have had broken necks or serious injuries had they been tied. I am not saying that no one should tie. I'm only relating my experience.

Time and patience is so important in training. Put the feelings of your animal first.

First Experience

AUTHOR'S NOTE

I know you've noticed I keep referring to the horse as he. It would be too time consuming and boring to write he or she each time.

I hope you will get as much joy out of your horses as I have. Now that I'm in a wheelchair, and my traveling days are over, I have such beautiful memories, plus pictures. My friends are still around. The young people I trained still keep in touch and come to visit. Even some of the older ones visit and keep in touch. I am just so blessed and thankful.

My tears are still at the surface when I think of my precious Cherokee, even though I've owned many other horses. His mane and tail were the same color as my hair -- blond-red. People sometimes teased me about dying either my hair or his to make sure they would match.

Blessings on all of you.

www.ingramcontent.com/pod-product-compliance
Lightning Source LLC
Chambersburg PA
CBHW022024090426
42739CB00006BA/275